Naturally Gourmet

Simple, plant-based recipes
that are healthy & delicious

KAREN HOUGHTON, RN, BSN

Hart Books

PO Box 2377, Fallbrook, CA 92088 · (800) 487-4278
www.NaturallyGourmet.com

Edited by Ken McFarland. Nutritional analysis by Eileen Kuninobu, RD. Designed by Mark Bond. Photography by Elena Gipson.
Additional Photography by Dan Houghton. Food stylist, Donna Hanson. Stock Photography by Jupiter Unlimited.
This book is not intended to diagnose or treat any medical conditions. Consult your physician before beginning any dietary plan.

TABLE OF CONTENTS

Bread of Life

Tasty Drinks

Just Deserts

Appendix

Foreword

Real living involves experiencing joy from all aspects of our lives. We have all heard the words of Socrates, "Thou shouldst eat to live; not live to eat." Many interpret this as a rejection of joyful eating. But I say that what we eat should greatly add to the joy of living. Sadly, many of us emphasize only short-term joy—that is, the pleasure of eating tasty food. I love tasty food, but there is an even greater joy—an enduring and long-lasting pleasure that comes only to those who eat abundantly of foods capable of healing and rejuvenating body, mind, and spirit.

Some believe that we must choose between the joys of food and the joys of optimal health. Karen Houghton has clearly shattered that myth. With this cookbook, she has shown that we can truly enjoy the pleasures of food. And we can do this while eating the very foods that are both the genesis of health and part of a divine solution against the majority of illnesses in this world.

Modern science now documents the presence of special properties in whole plant-based foods that can turn off disease-causing genes and turn on genes that promote health. But this transforming power of food is greatly enhanced when it is prepared to bring both long term and immediate joy.

Karen Houghton has done just that. With *Naturally Gourmet,*™ we can enjoy each day and anticipate the pleasure of each meal. Most important, *Naturally Gourmet* can help us anticipate many years of optimal health and the joys of a life well lived.

Wes Youngberg, DrPH, MPH, CNS
Clinical Preventionist & Nutrition Specialist
Director, Lifestyle Medicine Clinic & Wellness Center
Rancho Family Medical Group
Temecula, California

Introduction

As a young girl, I grew up in Wisconsin—the dairy state. When I went away to a boarding school for high school, I decided to become vegetarian. I ate a fair amount of cheese and dairy products when I eliminated meat from my diet. When I attended college, I took the nursing program at Andrews University. I enjoyed my classes but especially enjoyed my public health classes and the cooking classes we did for the community. My professor, Charlotte Hamlin, inspired us to share simple health principles with people and teach them how good nutrition can help to prevent disease. Those principles always stayed with me.

My attention was again drawn to this when my father developed type 2 diabetes. My parents attended Weimar Institute, a lifestyle program in California that specializes in reversal of diabetes. It really helped my dad. When I saw the effect that exercise and a plant-based diet had on my father, my conviction grew even stronger.

I have worked in hospitals, home health, and long-term care facilities. I wanted to help people but felt limited in what I could do and say.

When we moved to California, I decided to hold a small vegetarian cooking class in my home. I talked with our pastor at the time, and he encouraged me to do it in our church fellowship hall. So I advertised in the local paper, and we had around 100 people in attendance. For fifteen years I've been doing cooking classes in our community and always have a great response. I did a series of cooking classes in Phoenix for the It Is Written Television Ministry, and we had more than 120 people in attendance. So many people have failing health, and they are looking for an answer outside of drugs that have side effects and often only treat their symptoms. There is a place for medication, but if you can avoid it, why not?

When I started teaching these classes, I decided it was time to eliminate dairy products from my diet, as well. I found I actually felt better. I was highly motivated to make tasty food, because we have two sons who weren't going to be too interested in this if it didn't taste good! One thing I found—when you come under conviction with something in your diet, don't expect everyone else to have that same conviction. Just make your food tasty enough that they'll want to eat it!

I've learned over and over to experiment until you get a good result. I've also tried different cookbooks and found some really good recipes, which are in this book because I've been using them for years in my classes and wanted to share them with you too. (They are used with permission, of course!) The recipes in this book are some of our family favorites. I hope you enjoy them and that they will be a blessing to you and your family.

Karen Houghton

Karen Houghton, RN, BSN

Dedication

In thinking of to whom I would want to dedicate this book, my mother, Florence Szmanda, is the first one who came to my mind. Mom always made very tasty and healthy food for us. She set a table that looked appealing, with lots of color, and now we know that the more color there is on your plate, the better off you are. (She made me eat my green beans!)

As a young girl, I was the first in my home to become a vegetarian. Mom was the next in line to follow suit. Then, when Dad developed type 2 diabetes and my parents went to Weimar, Mom learned a whole new way to cook. She faithfully made healthy and tasty food. She would tell me, "You just have to adapt, adapt, adapt"—when you find a recipe that has ingredients you can't use, get creative and adapt.

So I want to thank my Mom, for all she's taught me and the wonderful example she's been to me all my life.

Helpful Hints

A few things I want to share with you will benefit you tremendously. First is the value of adding seeds and nuts to your diet.

Studies done on women eating a handful of nuts (i.e.: walnuts, pecans, almonds) more than five times a week found they had less than half the risk of coronary artery disease, as compared with those who rarely or never eat nuts.[1] Eat your nuts raw without the added fat and salt.

Brazil nuts are high in selenium, which is linked to a reduced risk for cancer and atherosclerosis. Eat at least three unsalted Brazil nuts a day. Just one provides 160 percent of our RDA for selenium.[2]

At all costs, avoid trans fats. Become a label reader. If something you pick off the shelf at the grocery store says "partially hydrogenated oils" or "hydrogenated vegetable oils," put it back. Don't bring it home. It clogs your arteries. You find these fats in things like peanut butter, pancake mix, crackers, cookies, etc. Also, check the labels in your pantry—you might be surprised. Trans fats contribute to type 2 diabetes. The Harvard School of Public Health found that every 2 percent increase in the number of calories from trans fat raises the risk of type 2 diabetes by 39 percent.[3] And the Rush Institute for Healthy Aging in Chicago found that eating significant amounts of "partially hydrogenated" vegetable oil increased one's risk of Alzheimer's disease by nearly two and one half times![4]

So what's so great about seeds? That's where lots of minerals are found—calcium, copper, iron, magnesium, selenium, and zinc, as well as vitamin E. Try different seeds on each given day—sunflower seeds, sesame seeds, pumpkin seeds—and make sure you get in flax seeds and chia seeds.

Flax seeds actually reduce inflammation in the body and help prevent blood clots. They lower cholesterol and triglycerides, help protect against deadly heart rhythms, and help arteries open wider.[5] That's a lot of benefits from those tiny seeds. You can't benefit from them, though, until you grind them up in a nut or seed grinder. Once they are ground, store them in the refrigerator for up to twenty-four hours. After twenty-four hours, they lose their nutritive value. So buy your seeds whole, not ground, and grind them yourself.

Chia seeds are also high in omega 3 fats and they don't have to be ground. Great for travel.

Remember each day—a handful of nuts, 2 - 3 Tbs of seeds, at least 8 glasses of water, 40 grams of fiber, 45 - 60 minutes of exercise, an attitude of gratitude and time in God's Word. You are well on your way to improved health. God bless you as you make strides to live a healthy and fulfilled life.

1. F. B. Hu. "Frequent Nut Consumption and Risk of Coronary Heart Disease in Women: Prospective Cohort Study," *BMJ*, 1998, 317:1314-1345.
2. *Food Science and Technology*, volume 42, issue 10, December 2009.
3. J. Salmeron. "Dietary Fat Intake and Risk of Type 2 Diabetes in Women," *American Journal of Clinical Nutrition*, 2001, 73:1019-1026.
4. M. C. Morris. "Dietary Fats and the Risk of Incident Alzheimer Disease," *Archives of Neurology*, February 2003, 60 (2): 194-200.
5. *Dr. Arnott's 24 Realistic Ways to Improve Your Health*. p. 33.

Fiber in Foods

These pages are intended to help you keep track of how much fiber you are getting in a day. I've made a little slogan to help you remember how important it is:

"If you want to lose weight and keep disease away, eat 40 grams of fiber, every single day!"

Remember, fiber is found only in plant foods—there is no fiber in meat or dairy products.

Try keeping track of just how much you are getting in a day. The average American gets about 10 grams a day—a far cry from where we should be.

This information will help you on your journey to better health.

The recipes in this book have the dietary fiber listed for each recipe. These fruits, vegetables, grains, beans, and nuts can supplement your recipe to bring your total up.

Fiber Content in Fruit

Fruit	Fiber	Fruit	Fiber
Avocado—1 med.	12 gm	Mango—1 C	3.0 gm
Papaya—1 med.	5.5 gm	Guava—1	3.0 gm
Pear—1 med.	5.5 gm	Kiwi—1	2.5 gm
Dried figs—5	5.0 gm	Cranberries—½ C	2.0 gm
Apple—1 med.	4.4 gm	Pineapple—1 C	2.0 gm
Raspberries—½ C	4.0 gm	Grapefruit—½	1.7 gm
Blackberries—½ C	4.0 gm	Peach—1 med.	1.6 gm
Shredded coconut—½ C	4.0 gm	Apricots—2	1.5 gm
Blueberries—1 C	3.6 gm	Date—1	1.5 gm
Prunes—3	3.5 gm	Cantaloupe—¼ sm.	1.4 gm
Strawberries—1 C	3.3 gm	Raisins—2 Tbs	1.3 gm
Orange—1	3.1 gm	Grapes—12	0.5 gm
Banana—1	3.1 gm		

Fiber Content in Vegetables*

Peas	4.4 gm
Brussels sprouts	4.0 gm
Corn	4.0 gm
Baked potato with skin—1 med.	4.0 gm
Sweet potatos/Yams	3.8 gm
Winter squash	3.0 gm
Hominy	3.0 gm
Carrots—1 raw or ½ C cooked	2.3 gm
Broccoli	2.5 gm
Spinach, collard greens	2.1 gm
Romaine lettuce—2 C	2.0 gm
Asparagus	2.0 gm
Green beans	2.0 gm
Okra or turnips	2.0 gm
Beets	1.6 gm
Bean sprouts	1.5 gm
Kale	1.3 gm
Zucchini, cooked & sliced	1.2 gm
Mushrooms, raw	1.0 gm
Summer squash	1.0 gm
Tomato—1 med.	1.5 gm
Lettuce	0.5 gm
Cauliflower, raw—1 floret	0.3 gm

Fiber Content in Legumes*

Navy beans	9.5 gm
Pinto beans	9.4 gm
Black beans	.7.5 gm
Lentils, pinto beans	.7.0 gm
Large lima beans	6.6 gm
Garbonzos	6.2 gm
Kidney beans	5.5 gm
Split peas, cooked	4.4 gm

Fiber Content in Nuts & Grains

Pearled barley—1 C, cooked	6.0 gm
Oats—1 C, cooked	4.0 gm
Brown rice—1 C, cooked	3.5 gm
Nuts/seeds—¼ C	3.0 gm
Ground flax seeds—1 Tbs	2.5 gm
Chia seeds—1 Tbs	2.5 gm
Peanut butter—1 Tbs	1.0 gm
Almond butter—1 Tbs	1.0 gm
Wheat germ—1 Tbs	1.0 gm

*(1/2 C cooked, unless noted)

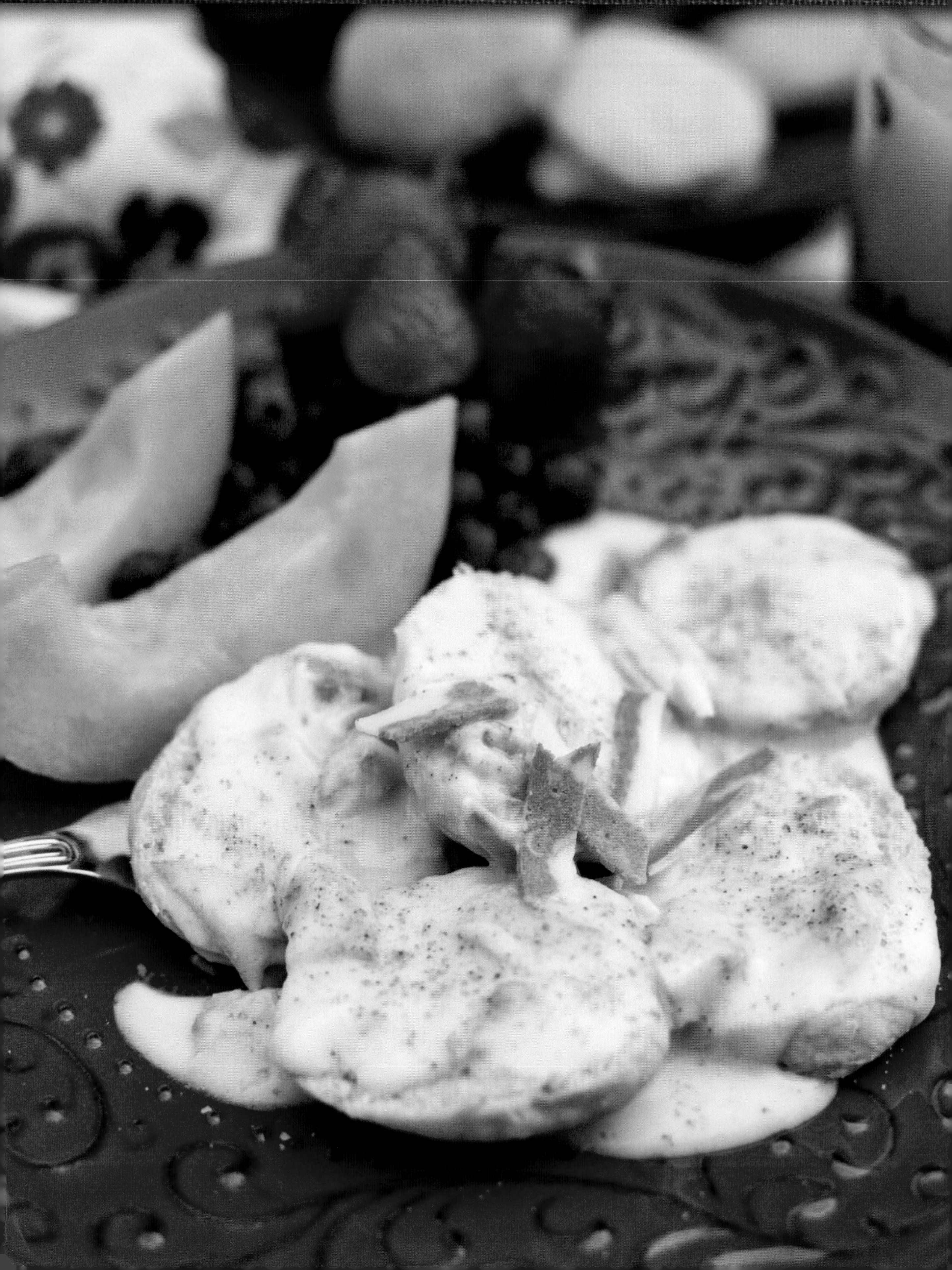

Biscuits & Gravy

Biscuits

3 C unbleached flour

1 C whole wheat flour

5 tsp Rumford baking powder

2 tsp salt

½ C extra-light olive oil

1 ¾ C water

Mix dry ingredients. Mix oil and water and add to dry ingredients. Roll the dough out on a floured board and use a biscuit cutter to make biscuits. Put the biscuits on an oiled cookie sheet. Bake at 400° for 20 minutes or until the top of the biscuits are lightly browned. Makes about 20 biscuits.

Gravy

3 C water

½ C washed raw cashews

½ C unbleached flour

Blend in blender until smooth.

Pour cashew gravy into a kettle. Cook over medium temperature until gravy thickens. Stir with wire whisk. Season with Lawry's seasoned salt or Mrs. Dash, if on a low-sodium diet. You can add Morningstar Farms Breakfast Patties, crumbled, Links, or chopped Stripples to the gravy, if desired. This gravy makes enough for 3-4 people.

Hint: If you want to increase the fiber, use whole wheat pastry flour for the gravy.
You will need to add plenty of fresh fruit to get your fiber quota in for the meal.

Biscuit Nutrition Facts (1 biscuit)
Calories 81, Fat 6 g, Saturated fat 1 g, Trans fat 0 g, Cholesterol 0 mg Sodium 454 mg, Carbohydrate 7 g, Dietary Fiber 1 g, Protein 1 g, Vitamin A 0%, Vitamin C 0%, Calcium 16%, Iron 3%

Gravy Nutrition Facts (1 serving = ¼ recipe)
Calories 141, Fat 7 g, Saturated fat 2 g, Trans fat 0 g, Cholesterol 0 mg, Sodium 6 mg, Carbohydrate 17 g, Dietary Fiber 1 g, Protein 4 g, Vitamin A 0%, Vitamin C 0%, Calcium 2%. Iron 10%

Brown Rice Pudding

2 C cooked brown rice

½ C chopped dates

½ C chopped raisins

½ C raw cashews

¼ tsp cinnamon

¼ C dried or fresh chopped pineapple

2/3 C or enough water to blend

1 Tbs honey or maple syrup

Preheat oven to 350°. Mix rice, dates, raisins, cinnamon, and pineapple in a bowl. Blend cashews, water, and honey until creamy. Add blended ingredients to rice mixture and combine well. Place in a well-oiled casserole dish and bake for 30 minutes. Serve warm with soymilk or pear cream (see p. 15).

Recipe adapted from *The Best of Silver Hills Cookbook.*

Nutrition Facts (1 serving = 1/2 recipe)

Calories 678, Fat 17 g, Saturated 3 g, Trans fat 0 g, Cholesterol 0 mg, Sodium 14 mg, Carbohydrate 129 g, **Dietary fiber 10 g,** Protein 13 g, Vitamin A 0%, Vitamin C 19%, Calcium 8%, Iron 26%

*For recipes highest in dietary fiber, the fiber content will appear in **bold** in Nutrition Facts boxes.

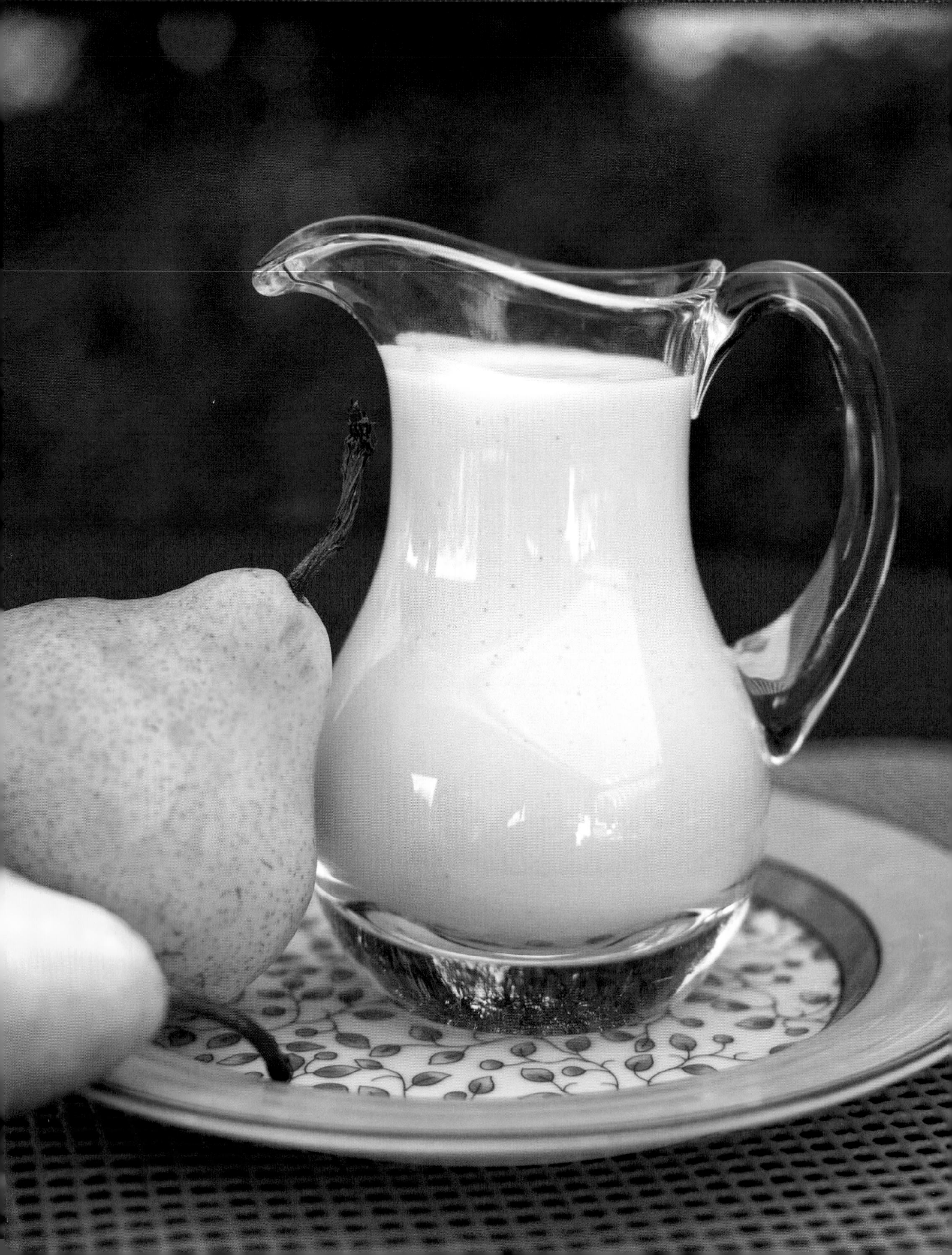

Pear Cream

½ C raw cashews

¼ tsp salt

1 tsp honey

1 qt canned pears in fruit juice

1 C fruit juice from canned pears or water

Place nuts in the blender. Add pear juice and blend until smooth. Add remaining ingredients until the milk is smooth and thick. Chill. Great on fruit salad, Brown Rice Pudding (p. 13), or other hot cereals.

Recipe from the
Best of Silver Hills Cookbook

Nutrition Facts (1 serving = 1/4 recipe)

Calories 214, Fat 7 g, Saturated fat 2 g,
Trans fat 0 g, Cholesterol 0 mg,
Sodium 155 mg, Carbohydrate 39 g,
Dietary Fiber 4 g, Protein 3 g, Vitamin A 0%,
Vitamin C 6%, Calcium 5%, Iron 10%

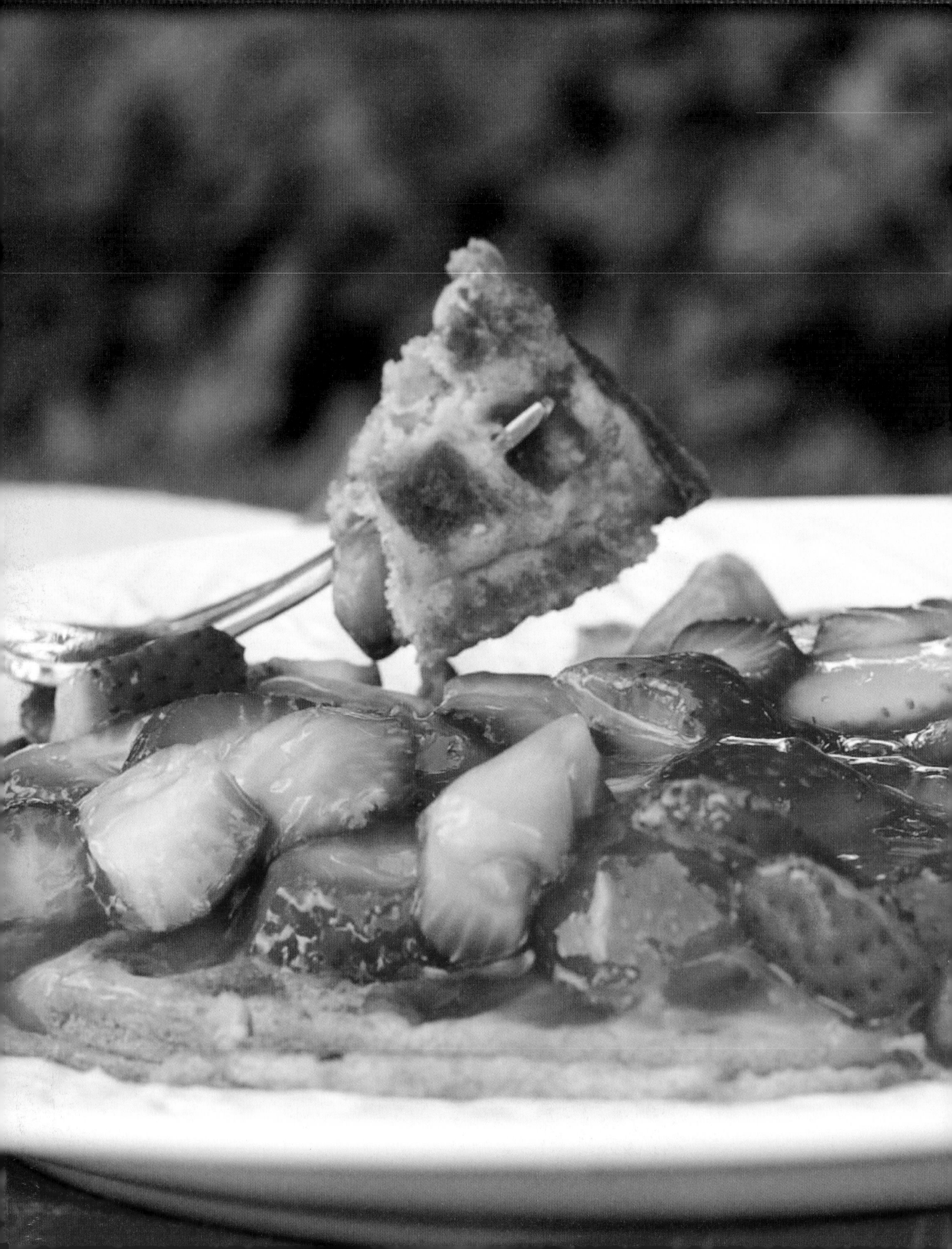

Waffles

1 C whole wheat pastry flour

½ C unbleached flour

½ C rolled oats

1 ½ tsp Rumford baking powder

2 ½ C soymilk

2 Tbs extra light olive oil

¼ C pure maple syrup

1 tsp vanilla

1 tsp cinnamon (optional)

Blend all ingredients in a blender. Let stand for a few minutes to thicken. Blend briefly before pouring onto a hot waffle iron. Spray waffle iron with olive oil spray before pouring waffle batter onto waffle iron. Cook for 10-12 minutes or until nicely browned. Makes 3 waffle squares of 4— or 12 waffles.

Hint: You can add 1 Tbs of ground flax seed to add another 2.5 gm of fiber to the total. Just blend with the other ingredients. You can sprinkle more on top of the nut butter you spread on the waffle and then top with fruit. (See pg. 35 for fruit topping recipe.)

Nutrition Facts (1 serving = 1 waffle)

Calories 129, Fat 4 g, Saturated 1 g, Polyunsaturated 1 g, Monounsaturated 2 g, Trans fat 0 g, Cholesterol 0 mg, Sodium 139 mg, Carbohydrate 21 g, Dietary fiber 2 g, Protein 5 g, Vitamin A 3%, Vitamin C 0%, Calcium 11%, Iron 8 %

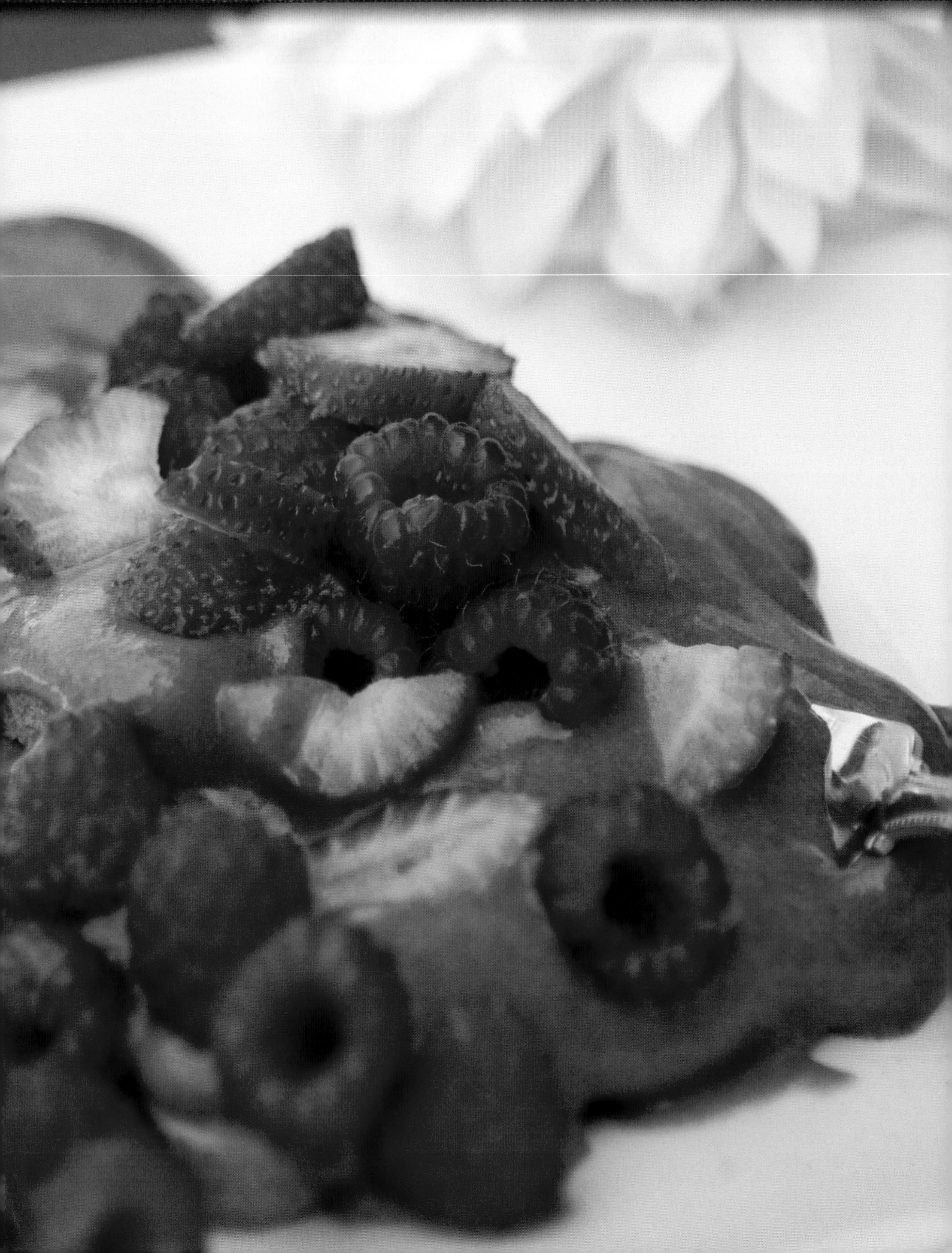

Strawberry-Raspberry Sauce

10 pitted dates

1 - 1 ¼ C pineapple or pineapple-orange juice

1 Tbs cornstarch

2 C sliced strawberries

2 C raspberries

Cook dates in a little water, unless you have a Vitamix or Blendtec blender. Blend dates, juice, and cornstarch in blender. Pour mixture into a kettle and bring to a boil. When thickened, stir in 2 C sliced strawberries and 2 C raspberries. You can mash them with a potato masher.

Put this topping on waffles, pancakes, or peanut-buttered toast. Topping is also great on cooked cereal or granola. You can add more fresh strawberries and raspberries as a topping. Serves 4.

Hint: I add some strawberries to the blender, as well, making the sauce red and creamy.

Nutrition Facts (1 serving = 1/4 recipe)

Calories 152, Fat 1 g, Saturated fat 0 g, Trans fat 0 g, Cholesterol 0 mg, Sodium 3 mg, Carbohydrate 38 g, **Dietary fiber 7 g**, Protein 2 g, Vitamin A 1%, Vitamin C 115%, Calcium 5%, Iron 7%

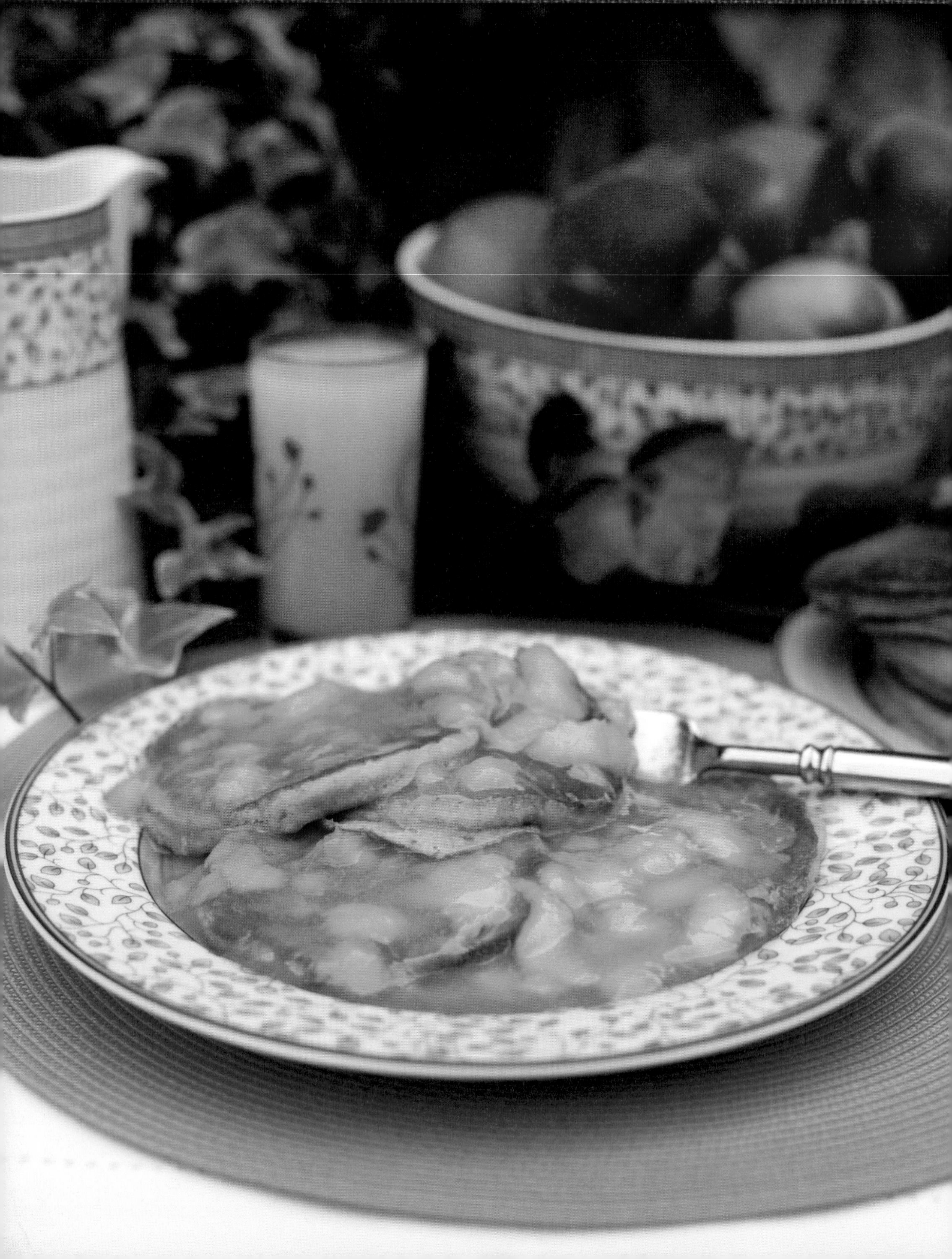

Blueberry Pancakes

Pancakes

¾ C whole wheat flour

½ C unbleached flour

1 ¼ C soymilk

1 ½ tsp vanilla

½ - 1 C blueberries

2 tsp baking powder

½ tsp cinnamon

1 Tbs light olive oil

1 Tbs honey

Mix the dry ingredients. Mix the liquid ingredients. Add the liquid to the dry ingredients and then add the blueberries.

Pour about ¼ C of batter onto a hot, oiled, non-stick skillet.
Turn the pancakes when they begin to bubble. Makes 15 pancakes.

Fruit Topping

1 quart frozen peaches defrosted or 5 - 6 fresh peaches (or fruit of your choice)

1 can frozen 100% apple juice or white grape juice

1 can of water   4 Tbs cornstarch

Mix the frozen juice, water, and cornstarch and bring to a slow boil until it thickens.
Then add the defrosted or fresh peaches.

Hint: This topping is wonderful with all kinds of different fruits. Blackberries have 8 g of fiber in one cup. I have used blueberries, peaches, strawberries, mixed berries, or mangos, and they all are tasty on top of pancakes or toast.

Pancake Nutrition Facts (1 pancake)

Calories 99, Fat 3 g, Saturated fat 0,
Polyunsaturated 1g, Monounsaturated 2g,
Trans fat 0, Cholesterol 0 mg, Sodium 136 mg,
Potassium 89 mg, Carbohydrate 16 g,
Dietary fiber 2 g, Sugars 2 g, Protein 3 g,
Vitamin A 2%, Vitamin C 1%, Calcium 10%,
Iron 7%

Topping Nutrition Facts
(1 serving = 1/6 recipe)

Calories 189, Fat 1 g, Saturated fat 0 g,
Trans fat 0 g, Cholesterol 0 mg,
Sodium 20 mg, Carbohydrate 47 g,
Dietary fiber 2 g, Protein 2 g, Protein 2 g,
Vitamin A 4%, Vitamin C 95%, Calcium 3%,
Iron 6%

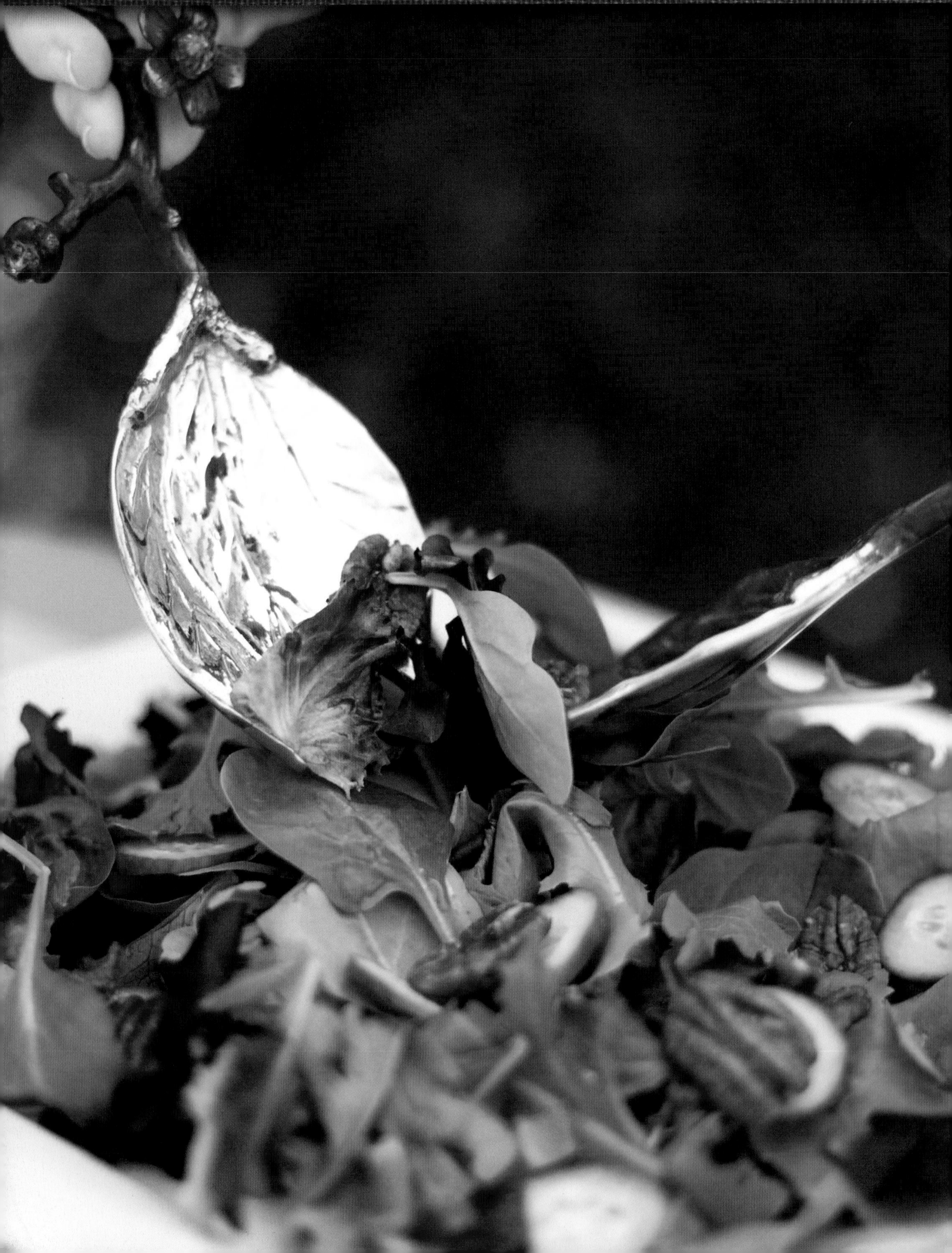

Mixed Greens Salad

Salad

1 bag mixed greens

2 Persian cucumbers, sliced

4 small yellow and/or orange bell peppers, sliced

¼ C dried black figs, diced

¼ C candied pecans

1 Bartlett pear, peeled and thinly sliced

Dressing

4 Tbs olive oil

2 ½ Tbs lemon juice, freshly squeezed

Salt to taste

In a salad platter combine greens, cucumbers, bell peppers, and figs. Just before serving, add lemon juice, olive oil, and salt to taste and toss. Sprinkle pecans on salad and place thin slices of pear on top. Enjoy! Serves 4-6.

Nutrition Facts (1 serving = 1/8 recipe)

Calories 206, Fat 15 g, Saturated 2 g, Polyunsaturated 3 g, Monounsaturated 9 g, Trans fat 0 g, Cholesterol 0 mg, Sodium 30 mg, Potassium 342 mg, Carbohydrate 20 g, Dietary fiber 4 g, Sugars 12 g, Protein 2 g, Vitamin A 74%, Vitamin C 137%, Calcium 4 %, Iron 7%

Bow Tie Pasta With Avocado

Salad

1 12 oz bow tie pasta

½ Tbs olive oil

2 avocados, diced

3 large Roma tomatoes, diced

2 green onions, chopped

4 - 5 Tbs fresh basil, chopped

Dressing

½ C olive oil

½ C fresh lemon juice

2 tsp salt

2 tsp oregano

2 tsp garlic powder

In a large pot bring salted water to a boil. Add the pasta and cook until done. Rinse pasta in cool water and drain. Add ½ Tbs olive oil and stir gently. Transfer to a serving platter.

Mix diced tomatoes, chopped green onions, diced avocados, and fresh basil, and pour some of the dressing over the vegetables. Pour avocado mixture over the pasta and toss gently. Add more dressing as desired. Delicious!

Salad yields 6 servings. Dressing yields 1 C or 8 servings (2 Tbs).

Using whole grain pasta will boost the fiber.

This recipe is adapted from the book
Depression, the Way Out, by Neil Nedley, MD.

Nutrition Facts (1 serving = 1/6 recipe)
Calories 327, Protein 8 g, Fat 12 g, Carbohydrate 46 g, Dietary fiber 5 g, Calcium 10 mg, Iron 7 mg, Sodium 9 mg

Dressing (1 serving = 2 Tbs) Calories 127, Fat 13.5 g, Carbohydrate 2 g, Calcium 8 mg, Sodium 582 mg

Coleslaw

Slaw

1 medium sized cabbage, chopped

1 - 2 shredded carrots

½ chopped onion

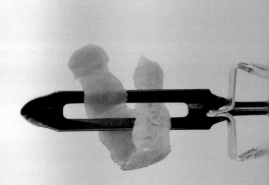

Dressing

3 - 5 Tbs Vegenaise

½ tsp salt

¼ tsp garlic powder

¼ tsp onion powder or a little more

Drizzle of olive oil

1 tsp lemon juice (fresh is best)

Add 1 - 2 Tbs water to thin it down

Mix dressing and pour over coleslaw.
Mix thoroughly. Garnish with extra carrot shreds.
Serves 6.

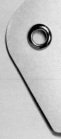

Nutrition Facts (1 serving = 1/6 recipe)

Calories 114, Fat 7 g, Saturated 1 g,
Trans fat 0 g, Cholesterol 0 mg, Sodium
287 mg, Carbohydrate 12 g, Dietary fiber 4 g,
Protein 2 g, Vitamin A 23%, Vitamin C 106%,
Calcium 8%, Iron 6%

Peas & Peanuts Salad

3 C peas, frozen

½ C onion, chopped

1 C jicama, sliced julienne style

½ C peanuts, dry-roasted, unsalted

¼ C sunflower seeds, dry-roasted, unsalted

¼ C pumpkin seeds

4 leaves romaine lettuce

1 Tbs green onion, chopped

1 cup Vegenaise

¼ tsp garlic salt

½ tsp onion salt

½ tsp Mrs. Dash Salt-Free Garlic and Herb Seasoning

Defrost one bag of frozen peas. Mix the peas, onions, and jicama together. Mix the peanuts, sunflower seeds, and pumpkin seeds together. Mix the Vegenaise, garlic salt, onion salt and Mrs. Dash Garlic and Herb Seasoning. Put the Romaine lettuce leaves or leaf lettuce on a plate.
When ready to serve, mix all the ingredients together and put in a mound on the lettuce.

Hint: If you want to make this ahead, don't add the seeds until ready to serve, or they won't be crisp.

Nutrition Facts (1 serving = 1/8 recipe)

Calories 341, Fat 27 g, Saturated 2 g, Trans fat 0 g, Cholesterol 0 mg, Sodium 389 mg, Carbohydrate 17 g, **Dietary fiber 6 g**, Protein 8 g, Vitamin A 9%, Vitamin C 16%, Calcium 4%, Iron 135

Southwest Salad

1 bag mixed salad greens (or 3 - 4 C)

1 can black beans, drained and rinsed

2 tomatoes, chopped

1 red bell pepper, chopped

2 C frozen corn, thawed or fresh kernels

1 avocado, chopped

¼ C cilantro, chopped

Layer ingredients in order listed. Top with salsa or drizzle ranch dressing on top. Serves 4.

Hint: You can also add sliced olives to this.

Nutrition Facts (1 serving = ¼ recipe)

Calories 253, Fat 9 g, Saturated 1 g,
Trans fat 0 g, Cholesterol 0 mg,
Sodium 470 mg, Carbohydrate 43 g,
Protein 12 g, **Dietary Fiber 11 g,** Vitamin A 58%,
Vitamin C 77%, Calcium 9%, Iron 20%

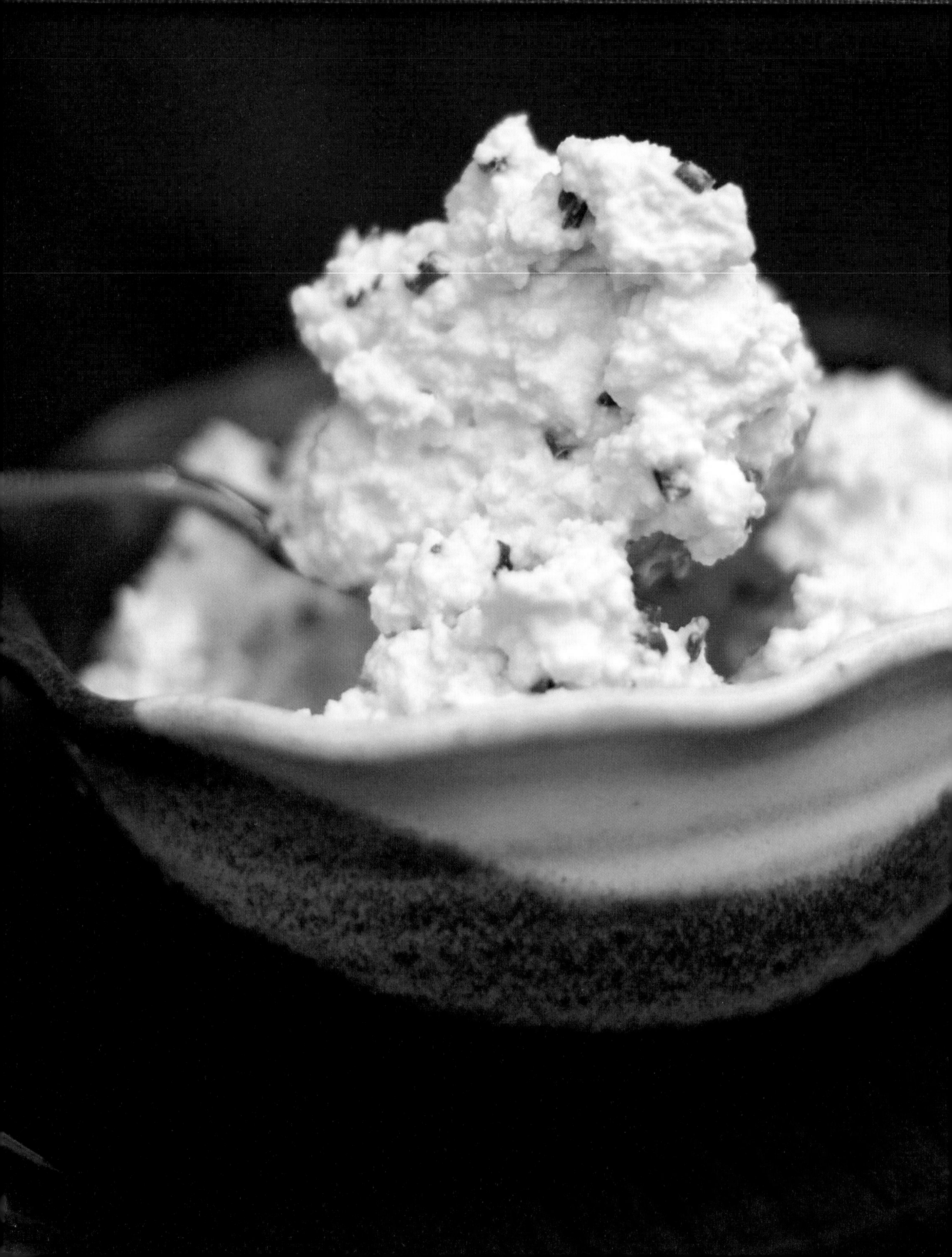

Tofu Cottage Cheese

4 C tofu, extra firm, water packed

2 ¼ tsp onion powder

¾ C Better Than Sour Cream

¼ tsp citric acid or 1 - 2 Tbs lemon juice

1 ½ tsp salt

½ tsp garlic salt

2 Tbs chives

Squeeze excess water out of the tofu by pressing tofu block between your hands. Crumble tofu in a bowl and add seasonings. Add citric acid to Better Than Sour Cream. Stir into tofu mixture. Mix in the chives. Makes 4 C. This recipe is from the Lifestyle Center of America.

Nutrition Facts (1 serving = 1/15 recipe)

Calories 91, Fat 6 g, Saturated 1 g, Trans fat 0 g, Cholesterol 0 mg, Sodium 367 mg, Carbohydrate 5 g, Dietary fiber 0 g, Protein 6 g, Vitamin A 0%, Vitamin C 2%, Calcium 11% , Iron 6%

Potato Salad

4 - 5 potatoes, peeled, cooked, and cubed

¾ C sliced green olives

4 green onions, chopped

2 pickles, diced (I prefer Bubbies brand)

1 carrot, shredded

4 - 5 Tbs Vegenaise

Salt to taste

Cube cooked potatoes. Add olives, green onions, carrot, and pickles. Stir in Vegenaise to moisten. Makes 6 servings.

Bubbie's pickles are found in the refrigerator section of a health food store. They are made with salt, garlic, dill, and spices. Very tasty.

Nutrition Facts (1 serving = 1/6 recipe)

Calories 197, Fat 9 g, Saturated Fat 0 g, Trans fat 0 g, Cholesterol 0 mg, Sodium 284 mg, Carbohydrate 28 g, Dietary fiber 3 g, Protein 3 g, Vitamin A 41%, Vitamin C 23%, Calcium 2%, Iron 4%

Veggie Lettuce Wraps

Romaine lettuce leaves

2 - 3 thinly sliced radishes

2 thinly sliced summer squash

1 red bell pepper, sliced in thin strips

1 avocado, diced

1 carrot, shredded

½ bunch cilantro, chopped

1 cucumber, chopped

Nutrition Facts (1 serving = 1/3 recipe)

Calories 262, Fat 19 g, Saturated 2 g,
Trans fat 0 g, Cholesterol 0 mg,
Sodium 213 mg, Carbohydrate 20 g,
Dietary Fiber 9 g, Protein 5 g, Vitamin A 155%,
Vitamin C 153%, Calcium 7%, Iron 10%

Put chopped veggies in a romaine lettuce leaf and top with ranch dressing.
Makes 2 - 4 lettuce wraps.

Salad Dressing

¼ C olive oil

¼ C fresh lemon juice

1 tsp salt

1 tsp garlic powder

1 tsp oregano

Mix all ingredients. If making ahead of time, you refrigerate it and then take it out soon enough so it will thin back down. The olive oil thickens when refrigerated.

Nutrition Facts (1 serving = 2 Tbs = ¼ recipe)

Calories 125, Fat 14 g, Saturated 2 g,
Polyunsaturated 2 g, Monounsaturated 10 g,
Trans fat 0 g, Cholesterol 0 mg,
Sodium 582 mg, Carbohydrate 2 g,
Dietary fiber 0 g, Protein 0 g, Vitamin A 1%,
Vitamin C 10%, Calcium 1%, Iron 2%

Tomato Florentine Soup

1 medium onion chopped

2 cloves garlic, minced

1 Tbs olive oil

2 1-lb cans tomato sauce, low sodium

1 16 oz can diced tomatoes

1 bay leaf

2/3 – 1 C soy creamer or ½ C raw cashews, blended in 1 C water

1 Tbs sucanat

1 tsp oregano

1 tsp basil

1 tsp garlic powder

1 tsp onion powder

2 C washed and chopped spinach

Sauté onion and garlic in olive oil in a kettle. Add tomatoes, tomato sauce, and seasonings. Simmer for ½ hour. Remove bay leaf and add spinach. Cook another 5 minutes. Serves 6.

Nutrition Facts (1 serving = 1/6 recipe)

Calories 150, Fat 7 g, Saturated 1 g, Trans fat 0 g, Cholesterol 0 mg, Sodium 343 mg, Carbohydrate 21 g, Dietary Fiber 4 g, Protein 4 g, Vitamin A 57%, Vitamin C 42%, Calcium 7%, Iron 12%

Cream of Fresh Vegetable Soup

1 ½ C chopped fresh vegetables (i.e.: peas, broccoli, asparagus)

1 Tbs olive oil

½ C onion, chopped

¼ C celery, diced

¼ C carrot, shredded

1 C fresh vegetables, diced

(I use about ¾ C asparagus and make the other ¼ C
with the other vegetables—love asparagus)

4 C water

2/3 C raw cashews

2 Tbs chicken style seasoning

1 tsp salt

½ tsp onion powder

¼ tsp celery salt

Steam 1 ½ C vegetables in a small amount of water until cooked. Place steamed vegetables in the blender and blend until smooth. Put blended vegetables in a bowl. Pour olive oil in a kettle and sauté onion, celery, and carrot. Then add 3 C of water and bring to a slow boil. Add blended vegetables and 1 C of diced fresh vegetables. Simmer for 5 minutes. Put cashews and 1 C of water and seasonings in the blender and blend until smooth. Slowly add to the soup and bring to a boil. This is a very tasty soup. Serves 4.

This recipe adapted from
The Best of Silver Hills Cookbook.

Nutrition Facts (1 serving = 1/4 recipe)

Calories 225, Fat 14 g, Saturated 3 g,
Polyunsaturated 2 g, Monounsaturated 9 g,
Trans fat 0 g, Cholesterol 0 mg,
Sodium 1300 mg, Carbohydrate 20 g,
Dietary fiber 4 g, Protein 7 g, Vitamin A 41%,
Vitamin C 35%, Calcium 5%, Iron 13%

Minestrone Soup

2 Tbs olive oil

½ C celery, chopped

½ C zucchini, sliced

½ C onion, chopped

½ C frozen cut Italian green beans

4 cloves of minced garlic

1 ½ cubes Organic Gourmet vegetable bouillon

4 C hot water

2 cans kidney beans

1 can small white beans

1 can garbonzo beans

1 14-oz can diced tomatoes

½ C carrots, sliced

½ C favorite marinara sauce

2 C baby spinach, chopped

½ C small shell pasta

1 Tbs fresh parsley, chopped

1 tsp dried oregano

1 tsp salt

½ tsp dried sweet basil

¼ tsp thyme

Heat the olive oil in a large kettle. Sauté the garlic, onion, celery, green beans, and zucchini until tender. Next, add the bouillon cubes, hot water, tomatoes, beans, carrots, and spices. Bring the soup to a boil and then simmer for 20 minutes. Next add the pasta and spinach and cook for another 20 minutes. Serves 8.

Hint: You can use whole grain pasta and boost the fiber content.

Nutrition Facts (1 serving = 1/8 recipe)
Calories 260, Fat 5g, Saturated 1 g, Polyunsaturated 1 g, Monounsaturated 3 g, Trans fat 0 g, Cholesterol 0 mg, Sodium 842 mg, Carbohydrate 43 g, **Dietary fiber 7 g,** Protein 12 g, Vitamin A 46%, Vitamin 18%, Calcium 12%, Iron 22%

Red Lentil Soup

1 C red lentils

4 C water

½ - 1 tsp salt

1 parsnip, diced

14-oz can petite diced tomatoes

¼ C fresh cilantro, chopped

½ - 1 tsp Mrs. Dash Southwest Chipotle seasoning blend

1 - 2 Tbs olive oil

1 carrot, diced

½ C onion, chopped

2 - 3 cloves garlic, minced

1 Tbs lemon juice

1 vegetable bouillon cube

Rinse the lentils in cold water. Drain and place in a kettle with 4 C water and the bouillon cube. Bring to a boil and cook for about ½ hour or until tender.

Sauté the carrot, parsnip, garlic, and onion until tender. Add the diced tomatoes and Mrs. Dash seasoning. Add the vegetables and seasonings to the soup and cook a little longer. Remove kettle from the stove and add the lemon juice and chopped cilantro. Serves 3 - 4.

This soup is a family favorite!

Nutrition Facts
(1 serving = 1/3 recipe)

Calories 385, Fat 9 g, Saturated 1 g, Trans fat 0 g, Cholesterol 0 mg, Sodium 801 mg, Carbohydrate 62 g, **Dietary fiber 13 g,** Protein 20 g, Vitamin A 89%, Vitamin C 46%, Calcium 12%, Iron 39%

Split Pea Soup

1 C split peas

4 C water

1 tsp salt

1 onion, chopped

1 - 2 carrots, grated

2 bay leaves

1 - 2 tsp minced garlic

1 Tbs olive oil (optional)

Cook split peas in salted water until soft—about ½ hour. Add onion, carrots, etc. and continue cooking until they are tender. Thin with water if the soup gets too thick.
Remove bay leaves before serving.
Serves 4.

Nutrition Facts (1 serving = ¼ recipe)

Calories 196, Protein 13 g, Fat 1 g,
Carbohydrate 37 g, **Dietary fiber 14 g,**
Calcium 45 mg, Iron 2 mg, Sodium 600 mg

Chili With Pesto

3-Bean Chili

½ C onion, chopped

1 carrot, chopped

1 can diced tomatoes

1 can garbanzos

1 can cannellini beans

1 can kidney beans

1 tsp salt

2 C water

Pesto Sauce

3 cloves minced garlic

3 Tbs pine nuts, chopped

1 C Italian parsley, chopped

¼ C olive oil

¼ tsp salt

Sauté onion and carrot with a little olive oil in large kettle until tender. Add tomatoes with liquid, 2 C water, 1 tsp salt, and bring to a boil. Rinse and drain garbanzos and beans and add to kettle.

Cook for another 5 minutes until heated. In a separate bowl, mix the garlic, pine nuts, parsley, olive oil and ¼ tsp salt. Spoon chili into bowls and top with pesto sauce. Serves 4.

Nutrition Facts (1 serving = 1/4 recipe)

Calories 515, Fat 20 g, Saturated 3 g, Polyunsaturated 5 g, Monounsaturated 12 g, Trans fat 0 g, Cholesterol 0 mg, Sodium 1890 mg, Carbohydrate 66 g, **Dietary Fiber 13 g**, Protein 19 g, Vitamin A 57%, Vitamin C 41%, Calcium 18%, Iron 35%

Karen's Veggie Sandwich

Sandwich

1 12-oz jar kalamata olives, pitted

1 cucumber, thinly sliced

1/2 - 1 stalk celery, thinly sliced

Fresh baby spinach leaves

1 loaf whole wheat French or foccacia vvbread

1 - 2 radishes, thinly sliced

1 red bell pepper, sliced into thin strips

Green onions, chopped

(Ideal bread is foccacia—it's a flat bread and won't need to be scooped out. French bread is quite thick, so that's why some of it will need to be scooped out.)

Dressing

½ C olive oil

2 tsp garlic powder

1 tsp oregano

1/3 C lemon juice

1 tsp salt

Slice loaf of bread horizontally. In food processor grind up the kalamata olives into an olive paste. Scoop out part of the lower half of the loaf of bread. Then spread the olive paste over the lower half the bread. Put cucumber slices on top of the olive spread and then layer the radishes, celery, and red pepper slices, and end with fresh baby spinach leaves. Mix dressing and pour over the inside top of loaf. You won't need the whole amount of the dressing. Place the top of loaf over the lower half and slice into 4 - 5 segments for sandwiches. This is one of our favorite sandwiches. Goes great with home-made soup.

Preparation Tip: If you want to make the sandwiches ahead the same day, wrap them in plastic wrap until ready to eat.

Nutrition Facts (1 serving = 1/5 recipe)

Calories 717, Fat 42 g, Saturated 4 g, Trans fat 0 g, Cholesterol 0 mg, Sodium 2172 mg, Carbohydrate 74 g, Dietary fiber 4 g, Protein 13 g, Vitamin A 30%, Vitamin C 76%, Calcium 7%, Iron 25%

SANDWICHES

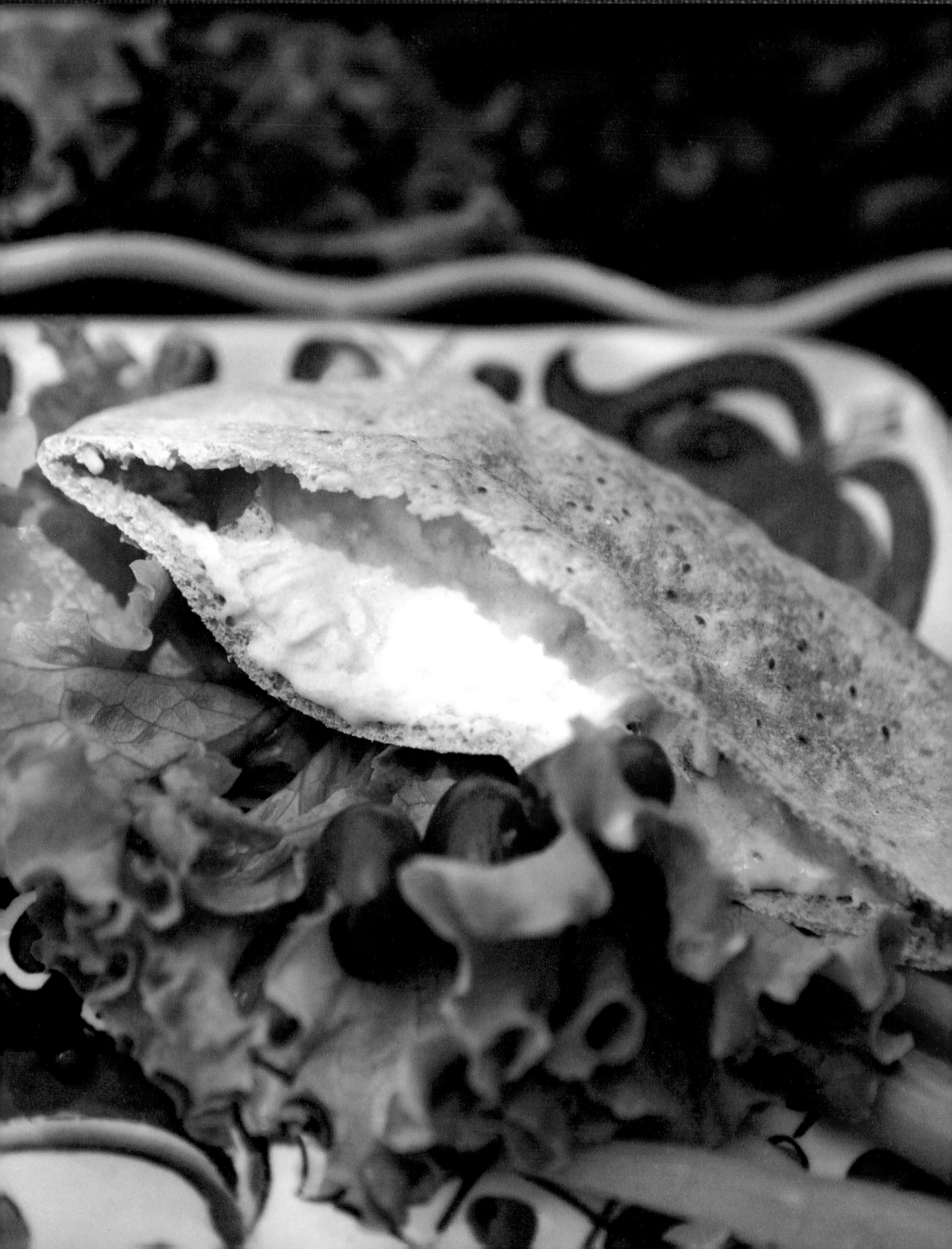

Pita Bread Sandwich

1 whole wheat pita pocket

2 - 3 Tbs hummus

1 tomato, chopped

2 Tbs chopped olives

1 green onion, chopped

½ avocado, diced

2 - 3 Tbs tzadzeki—also known as creamy cucumber sauce

Cut whole wheat pocket bread in half. Spread the hummus inside. Stuff the pocket with the chopped tomato, olives, green onion, and avocado. Top with tzadzeki.

Makes 2 sandwiches.

Hint: We like to use Lawry's seasoned salt or Tony's to sprinkle on the hummus.

Nutrition Facts (1 sandwich = 1/2 recipe)

Calories 338, Fat 24 g, Saturated 4 g,
Trans fat 0 g, Cholesterol 0 mg,
Sodium 321 mg, Carbohydrate 29 g,
Dietary fiber 6 g, Protein 6 g, Vitamin A 6%,
Vitamin C 19%, Calcium 4%, Iron 10%

SANDWICHES

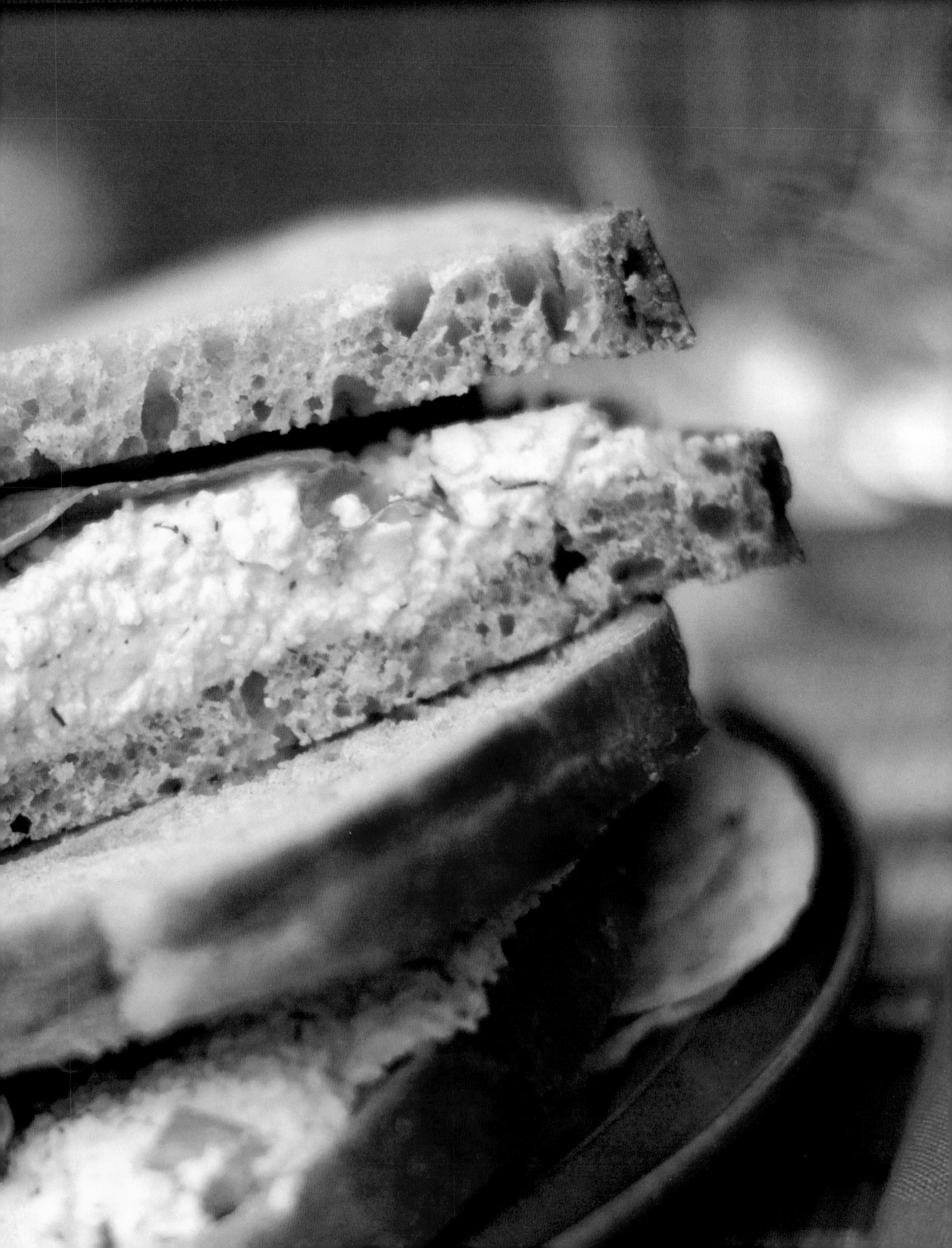

Tofu Egg Salad

1 pound tofu, drained

4 Tbs Vegenaise

Chopped celery

Chopped green onions

Chopped pickles

1 tsp turmeric

1 tsp dill weed

1/2 tsp salt (or to taste)

Nutrition Facts (1 serving = 1/6 recipe)

Calories 126, Protein 6 g, Fat 10 g, Carbohydrate 5 g, Dietary fiber 1 g, Calcium 136 mg, Iron 2 mg, Sodium 303 mg

Mash tofu with a fork. Mix ingredients together. Add chopped celery, green onions, and chopped dill pickles to mixture. Great on whole grain toast. Serves 6.

Hint: Adding veggies will boost the fiber, and if you use Oroweat Double Fiber bread, there are 12 gm of fiber in 2 slices.

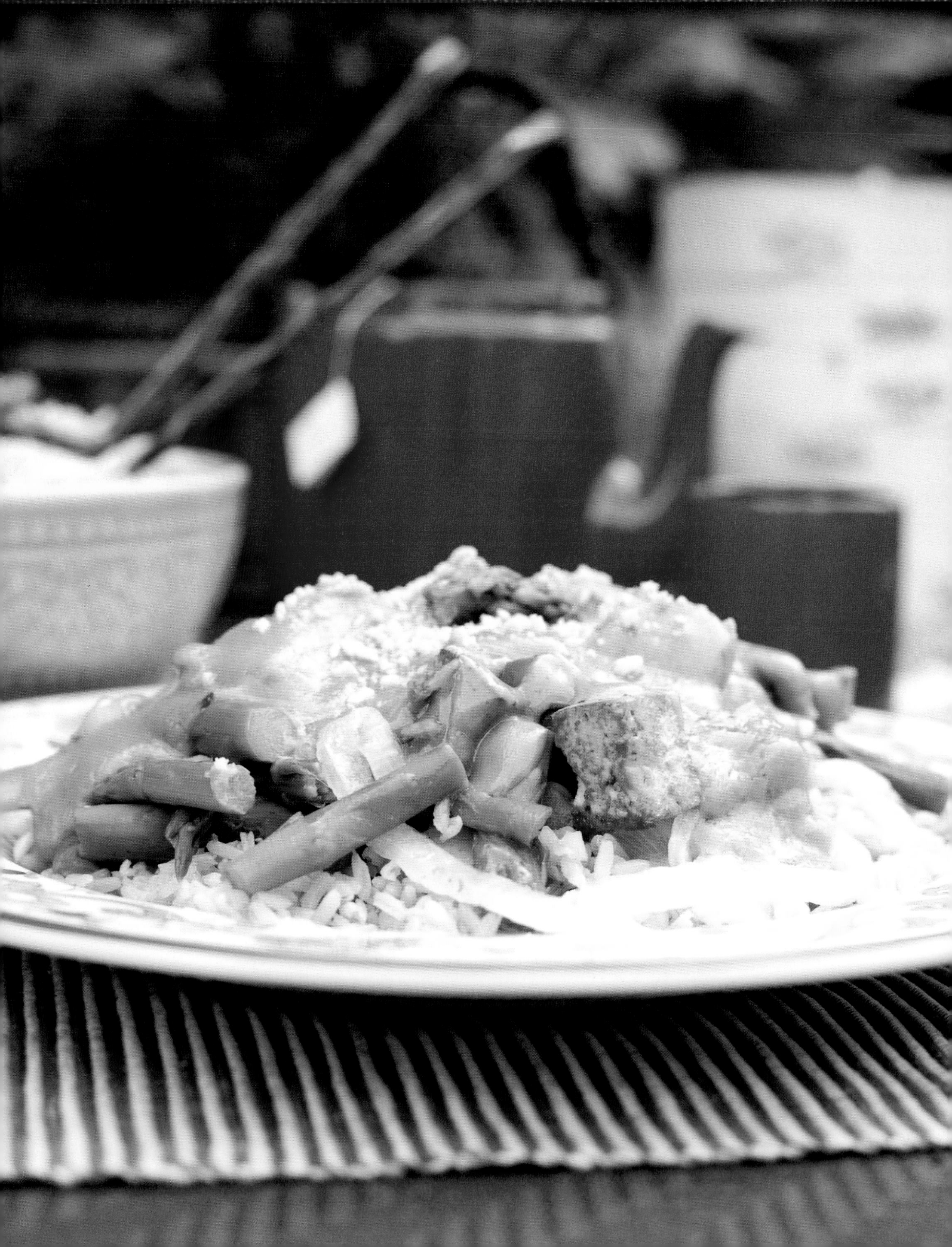

A Taste of Thai

2 bunches asparagus, steamed

½ - 1 onion, cut and sautéed

1 firm water pak tofu, cubed

3 Tbs olive oil, 3 Tbs soy sauce, minced garlic, and salt to taste

In a frying pan, drizzle olive oil, and heat the oil to hot. Add the cubed tofu and fry until it's nicely browned. Then add the soy sauce and minced garlic and cook a little longer to season the tofu. Set it aside. (If you prefer to bake the tofu, you can drizzle 1 Tbs olive oil, 1 Tbs soy sauce, then add garlic and salt and mix gently in a bowl—then pour onto a baking sheet. Bake at 350° for about 20 minutes, until nicely browned.)

Thai Peanut Sauce

1 can light coconut milk

¾ C creamy peanut butter

½ tsp salt

1 - 2 Tbs fresh lemon juice

¼ C water

1/8 tsp red curry paste (optional)

1/3 C sucanat or more to taste

Nutrition Facts, Fried (1 serving=1/5 recipe)

Calories 574, Fat 38 g, Saturated 11 g, Trans fat 0 g, Cholesterol 0 mg, Sodium 802 mg, Carbohydrate 40 g, **Dietary fiber 11 g**, Protein 25 g, Vitamin A 20%, Vitamin C 33%, Calcium 27%, Iron 60%

Nutrition Facts, Baked (1 serving=1/5 recipe)

Calories 523, Fat 33, Saturated 11 g, Trans fat 0 g, Cholesterol 0 mg, Sodium 562 mg, Carbohydrate 39 g, **Dietary fiber 11 g**, Protein 25 g, Vitamin A 20%, Vitamin C 33%, Calcium 27%, Iron 59%

Heat coconut milk in a kettle on low until it simmers. Then add peanut butter, sucanat, salt, and red curry paste. Simmer on low heat until sauce is well blended and begins to thicken.

Stir together steamed asparagus and sautéed onions. Put cooked brown rice on the plate, then asparagus, onions, and fried tofu. Top with peanut sauce and a sprinkle of unsalted, chopped peanuts.

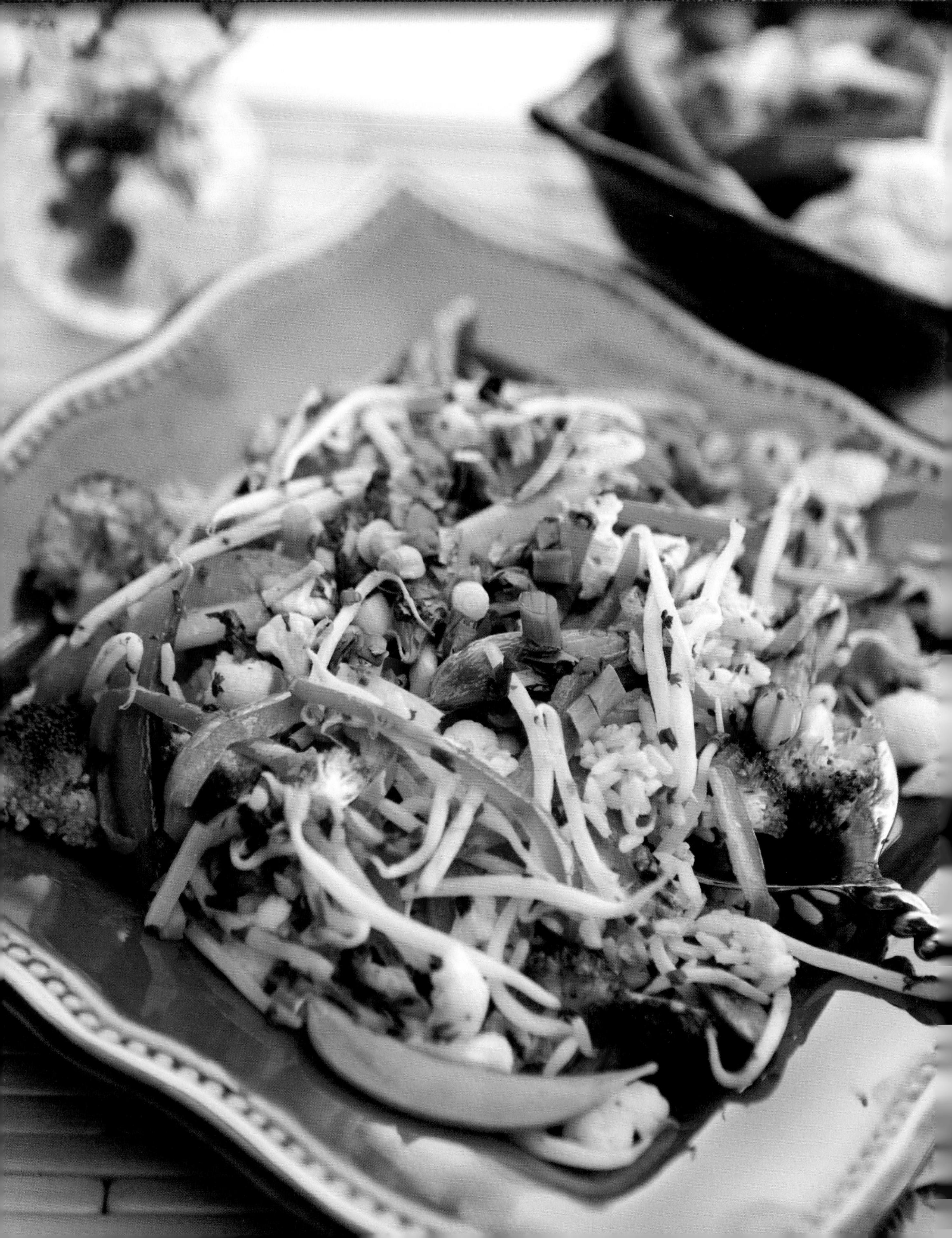

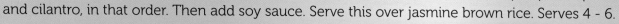

Broccoli Stir Fry

1 ½ C cauliflower florets

1 ½ C broccoli florets

1 ½ C pea pods

1 red bell pepper, sliced in thin strips

1 stalk celery, chopped

4 green onions, chopped

A handful of bean sprouts

½ bunch of cilantro, chopped

Olive oil

3 - 4 cloves of garlic minced

1 Tbs oregano

1 - 2 Tbs light soy sauce

Sauté fresh garlic and herbs in olive oil. Then add pepper, cauliflower, broccoli, pea pods, sprouts, and cilantro, in that order. Then add soy sauce. Serve this over jasmine brown rice. Serves 4 - 6.

Nutrition Facts (1 serving = 1/5 recipe)
Calories 71, Fat 3 g, Saturated .5 g,
Polyunsaturated .5 g, Monounsaturated 2 g,
Trans fat 0 g, Cholesterol 0 mg,
Sodium 206 mg, Carbohydrate 10 g,
Dietary fiber 3 g, Protein 3 g, Vitamin A 13%,
Vitamin C 107%, Calcium 6%, Iron 10%

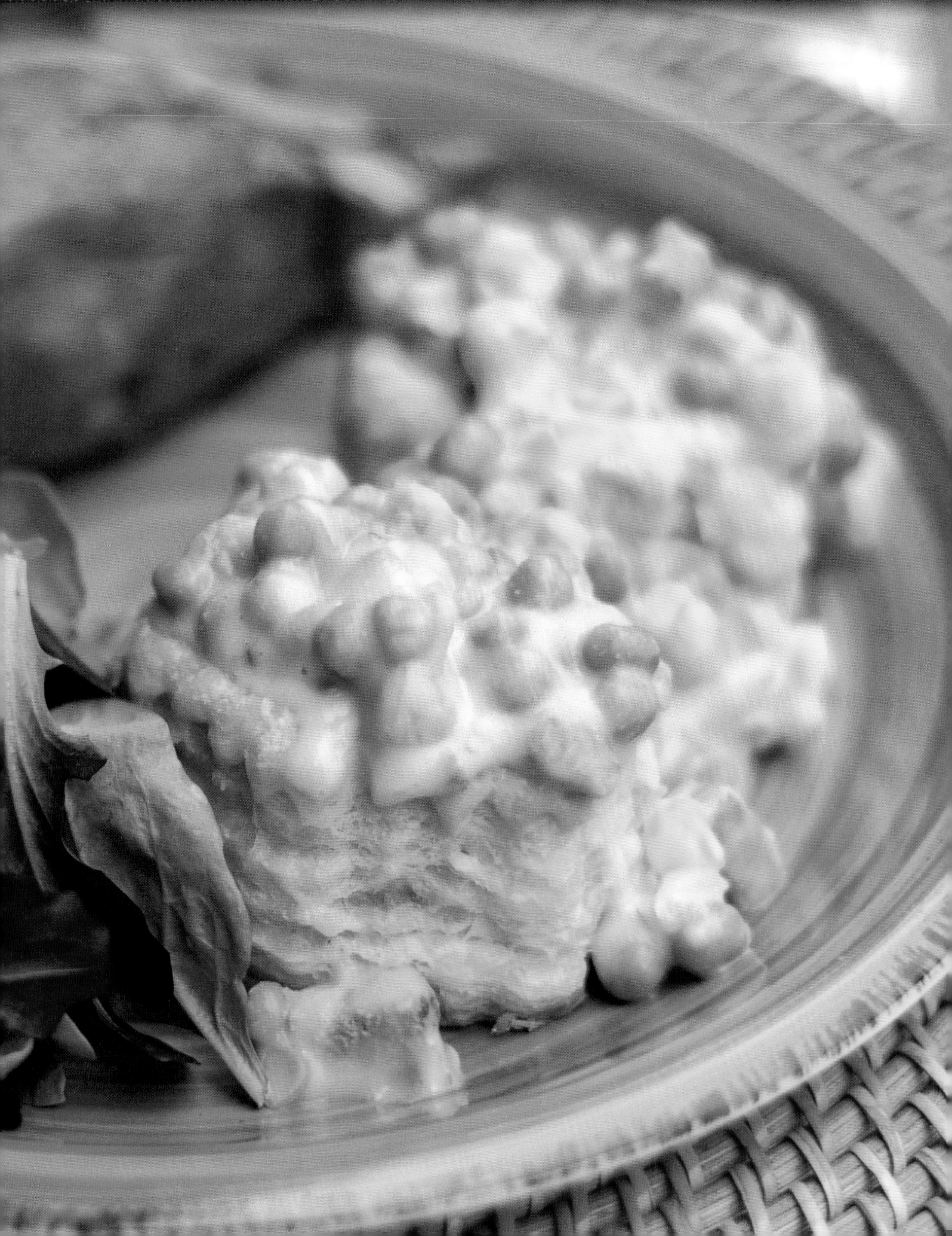

Chicken à La King

1 pkg frozen peas and carrots, cooked

½ C onion diced and sautéed

1/2 C sweet red pepper, diced and sautéed

Cashew Gravy

3 C water

½ C raw, washed cashews

½ C unbleached flour

Liquify the cashews and water in the blender until smooth.
Then add the flour to the blender and blend again.
Next, add to the cashew milk:

1 ½ tsp vegetarian chicken seasoning

¼ tsp garlic powder

½ tsp soy sauce or liquid aminos

1 ½ tsp salt

1 tsp onion powder

Nutrition Facts (1 serving = 1/9 recipe)

Calories 125, Fat 9 g, Saturated 1 g, Trans fat 0 g, Cholesterol 0 mg, Sodium 21 mg, Carbohydrate 10 g, Dietary fiber 3 g, Protein 3 g, Vitamin A 3%, Vitamin C 72%, Calcium 6%, Iron 8%

Cook mixture until thickened like gravy. Then add
the sautéed onions, sweet red pepper, and cooked
peas and carrots. Add diced tofu that's been sautéed (or baked) and slightly
browned, or 1 can diced Worthington FriChik. (FriChik is a soy meat substitute and can be
purchased at health food stores.) Serves 8.

Serving Tip: Pour chicken gravy over cooked brown rice or baked Pepperidge Farm pastry shells.
Also good over whole grain toast.

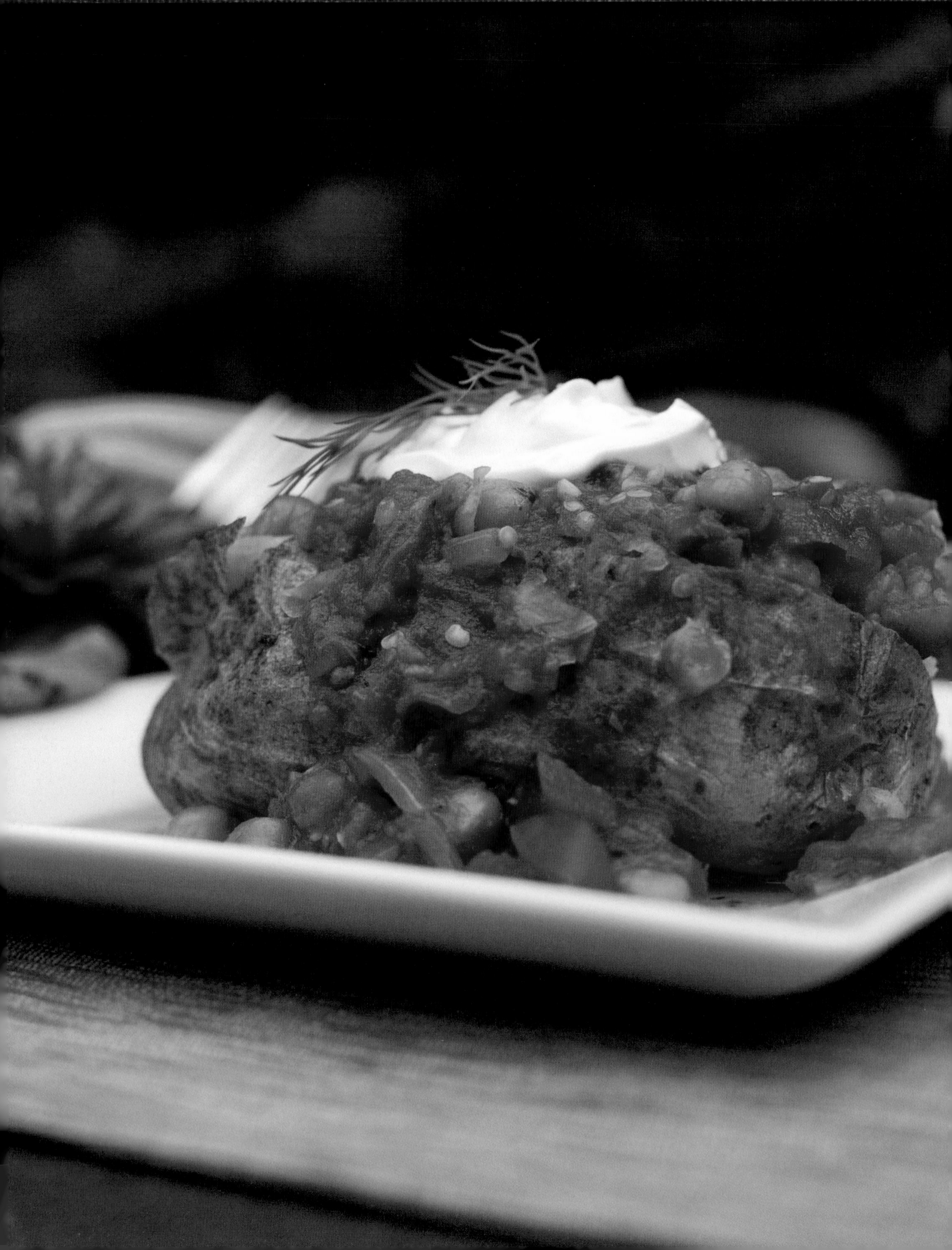

Eggplant & Garbanzo Ratatouille

4 cloves garlic, chopped

½ C onion, chopped

1 - 2 Tbs olive oil

½ tsp Italian seasoning

1 small eggplant, chopped

3 C fresh or canned diced tomatoes

¾ C canned garbonzos, rinsed and drained

½ C chopped fresh basil

Nutrition Facts (1 serving = ¼ recipe)

Calories 139, Fat 6 g, Saturated 1 g, Polyunsaturated 1 g, Monounsaturated 4 g, Trans fat 0 g, Cholesterol 0 mg, Sodium 143 mg, Carbohydrate 20 g, Dietary fiber 5 g, Protein 4 g, Vitamin A 10%, Vitamin C 30%, Calcium 5%, Iron 8%

Sauté the garlic, onion, and eggplant in the olive oil until tender. Add the seasoning, diced tomatoes, and garbanzos. Salt to taste. Pour over cooked brown rice, penne pasta, or a baked potato. Serves 4.

Veggie Fajitas

2 zucchini, sliced thin

2 summer squash, sliced thin

1 red bell pepper, sliced in strips

1 yellow bell pepper, sliced in strips

1 orange bell pepper, sliced in strips

1 small onion, sliced

1 carrot, sliced in thin strips

½ pkg Morningstar Farms Meal Starters Chik'n Strips (optional)

1 - 2 Tbs olive oil

Whole wheat tortillas

½ C Vegenaise or less

1/3 C cilantro, chopped

¼ tsp garlic powder

Nutrition Facts (1 serving = ¼ recipe)

Calories 407, Fat 27 g, Saturated 2g, Trans fat 0 g, Cholesterol 0 mg, Sodium 479 mg, Carbohydrate 39 g, **Dietary fiber 17 g**, Protein 13 g, Vitamin A 43%, Vitamin C 327%, Calcium 11%, Iron 14%. (When you use the La Tortilla Soft Wraps, you really boost the fiber, as their wraps have 12 - 13 gm of fiber in one wrap.)

Sauté veggies in olive oil until tender. Mix the Vegenaise with the chopped cilantro and garlic powder. Spread the Vegenaise mixture on a whole wheat tortilla, top with the sautéed veggies, and season with salt, Spike, Mrs. Dash, or Frontier Mexican seasoning to taste. Serves 4. (You can use other veggies in these, as well.)

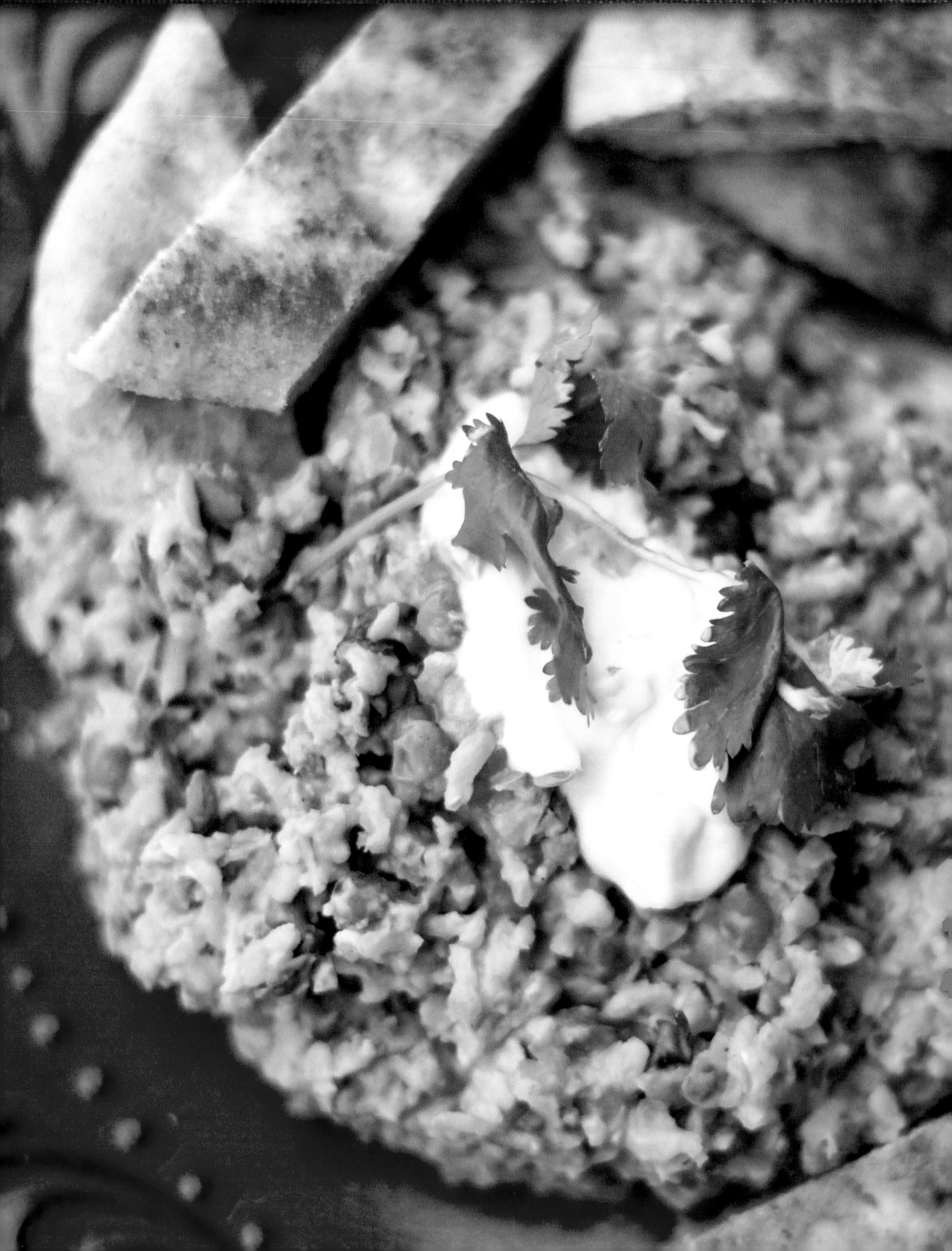

Indian Lentils & Rice

1 Tbs olive oil

1 C onion, thinly sliced

1 C uncooked jasmine brown rice

1 Tbs curry powder

1 ½ tsp salt

4 C water

1 C lentils

1 C fresh cilantro, chopped

½ C Better Than Sour Cream

Sauté onions in olive oil in kettle. Add rice, curry powder, and salt, and sauté for 1 minute. Add water and lentils and bring to a boil.

Cover, reduce heat, and simmer for 1 hour. Remove from heat and add cilantro and Better Than Sour Cream. This is good with naan (Indian bread), and a salad. Serves 3 - 4.

Nutrition Facts (1 serving = ¼ recipe)
Calories 477, Fat 11 g, Saturated 3 g,
Trans fat 0 g, Cholesterol 0 mg,
Sodium 1050 mg, Carbohydrate 78 g,
Dietary Fiber 18 g, Protein 18 g, Vitamin A 6%,
Vitamin C 11%, Calcium 6%, Iron 27%

Lentil Roast

1 ½ C cooked lentils

1 C soymilk

¼ C extra light olive oil

½ C onion, chopped

½ C pecan meal

1 tsp garlic powder

1 ½ C cornflakes

Salt to taste

Mix and put in oiled casserole dish. Bake at 350° for 45 minutes. Roast can be topped with ketchup, gravy, or barbecue sauce—also good just plain. Serves 6.

Note: if you can't find pecan meal, just grind pecans up in a food processor or blender.

Nutrition Facts (1 serving = 1/6 recipe)

Calories 259, Protein 7 g, Fat 17 g, Carbohydrate 22 g, Dietary fiber 5 g, Calcium 70 mg, Iron 5 mg, Sodium 13 mg

Mushroom Gravy

1/3 C canned mushrooms, with the juice

2 Tbs cornstarch

1 Tbs vegetarian beef seasoning

¾ tsp salt

2/3 C raw cashews

2 C water

Blend water and cashews until creamy. Add vegetarian beef seasoning, salt, and cornstarch and blend well. Add mushrooms and blend briefly. Pour the gravy into a kettle and cook until thickened. Stir frequently. Serves 6.

Nutrition Facts (1 serving = 1/6 recipe)

Calories 80, Fat 5 g, Saturated 1 g, Cholesterol 0 mg, Sodium 324 mg, Carbohydrate 7 g, Dietary fiber 1 g, Protein 2 g, Vitamin A 0%, Vitamin C 0%, Calcium 2%, Iron 6%

Simple Asian Stir Fry

4 mushrooms, sliced

1 red pepper, sliced

1 green pepper, sliced

1 stalk celery, sliced

1 carrot, sliced

½ onion, sliced

2 cloves garlic, minced

1 package tofu, cubed

5 Tbs olive oil

6 Tbs soy sauce

1 tsp cornstarch

4 oz water

Drain and cut tofu. Heat frying pan on high and fry tofu with 3 Tbs of olive oil, 3 Tbs of soy sauce, and garlic to season. Then stir fry vegetables in frying pan in 2 Tbs of olive oil. Add garlic, onions, carrots, bell peppers, celery, and mushrooms. Cook to desired tenderness. Season with 3 Tbs of soy sauce.

Mix 1 tsp of cornstarch with 4 oz of water. Add vegetables to tofu and cornstarch mixture. Cook to thicken a little. Serve hot over steamed brown jasmine rice.

Nutrition Facts (1 serving = ¼ recipe)

Calories 627, Fat 24 g, Saturated 3 g, Polyunsaturated 2 g, Monounsaturated 12 g, Trans fat 0 g, Cholesterol 0 mg, Sodium 935 mg, Potassium 331 mg, Carbohydrate 82 g, Dietary fiber 4 g, Sugars 4 g, Protein 21 g, Vitamin A 29%, Vitamin C 87%, Calcium 18%, Iron 14%

Stuffed Shells

Tofu Cottage Cheese

4 C tofu, extra firm, water packed

1 ½ tsp salt

2 ¼ tsp onion powder

½ tsp garlic salt

¾ C Better Than Sour Cream

2 Tbs chives

1/8 tsp citric acid or 1 - 2 Tbs lemon juice

Squeeze excess water out of tofu by pressing tofu block between hands. Crumble tofu in a bowl and add seasonings. Add citric acid to "sour cream." Stir into tofu mixture. Yield 4 C.

1 - 2 jars green and black olive spaghetti sauce

1 box jumbo shells

Cook jumbo shells. Spread a thin layer of spaghetti sauce in bottom of baking dish. Stuff cooled and rinsed shells with tofu cottage cheese. Place shells in baking dish. If the sauce is too chunky, you can blend it briefly. Pour over stuffed shells. Bake at 350° for 30 minutes. Makes 35 shells.

Hint: I like the Barilla green and black olive spaghetti sauce.

Nutrition Facts (1 serving = 2 shells)

Calories 177 (calories from fat 51), Fat 6 g, Saturated 1 g, Cholesterol 0 mg, Sodium 688 mg, Carbohydrate 23 g, Dietary fiber 2 g, Sugars 3 g, Protein 8 g, Vitamin A 2%, Calcium 9%, Iron 8%

Vegetable Pot Pie

1 potato, cubed

1 block baked or fried tofu, cubed, or 1 can Lowfat FriChik, diced

2 carrots, sliced

¼ C onion, diced

1 stalk celery

½ C frozen lima beans

1 tsp salt

½ -1 recipe mushroom gravy (p. 73)

1 recipe single pie crust (p. 113)

Cook vegetables until almost tender in ¼ C water. Add tofu or FriChik, and mushroom gravy. Pour gravy and vegetables into casserole dish. Top with pie crust. Bake at 425° for 30 minutes. Serves 8. If using tofu, cut into small cubes and then fry in a hot pan with olive oil and salt, and brown. Cool, then add to the rest of the vegetables.

(8 servings includes gravy and crust)

Nutrition Facts (1 serving = 1/8 recipe)
Calories 376, Protein 10 g, Fat 19 g, Carbohydrate 42 g, Dietary fiber 4 g, Calcium 91 mg, Iron 3 mg, Sodium 1138 mg

Roasted Cauliflower & Broccoli

4 - 5 C of broccoli, stems trimmed

4 - 5 C of cauliflower, stems trimmed

5 - 6 cloves of garlic, cut in long strips

Salt to taste

3 - 4 Tbs extra virgin olive oil

1 fresh lemon

Wash vegetables and trim stems. Put veggies in a bowl and add garlic strips and salt, and drizzle olive oil on top. Mix veggies well and put on a cookie sheet and bake at 425° for 20 - 25 minutes until tender. After baking, squeeze the juice from a fresh lemon and drizzle over the vegetables. Serves 6 - 8.

Nutrition Facts (1 serving = 1/7 recipe)

Calories 91, Fat 7 g, Saturated 1 g, Polyunsaturated 1 g, Monounsaturated 5 g, Trans fat 0 g, Cholesterol 0 mg, Sodium 32 mg, Carbohydrate 7 g, Dietary fiber 2 g, Protein 3 g, Vitamin A 10%, Vitamin C 102%, Calcium 5%, Iron 5%

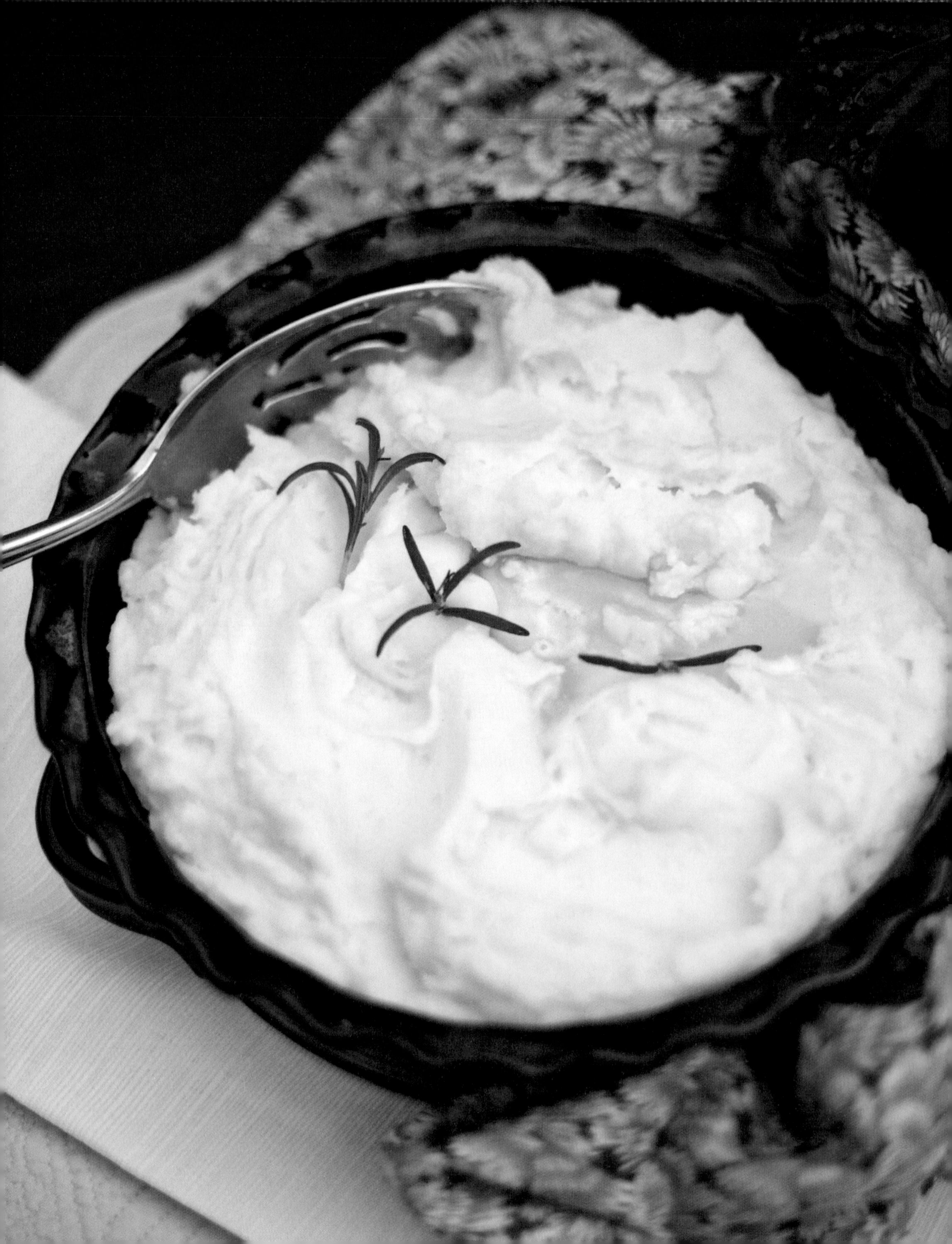

Whipped Potatoes

4 - 5 potatoes, peeled and cooked

Water from cooked potatoes

½ tub or more of Better Than Sour Cream

Salt to taste

Peel potatoes and cut into quarters. Cook in enough water to cover potatoes. Remove potatoes and put in a bowl. Add a little potato water, some Better Than Sour Cream, and salt. Mix with a potato masher or use an electric mixer and whip until smooth and fluffy. Add more sour cream as needed. When ready to serve, you can add 1 - 2 Tbs of Earth Balance margarine on top. These can be prepared the day ahead and refrigerated, then reheated. They are best though, the day you make them.

Nutrition Facts (1 serving = 1/5 recipe)

Calories 249, Fat 6 g, Saturated 3 g, Trans fat 0 g, Cholesterol 0 mg, Carbohydrate 44 g, Dietary fiber 4 g, Protein 5 g, Vitamin A 0%, Vitamin C 50%, Calcium 3%, Iron 9%

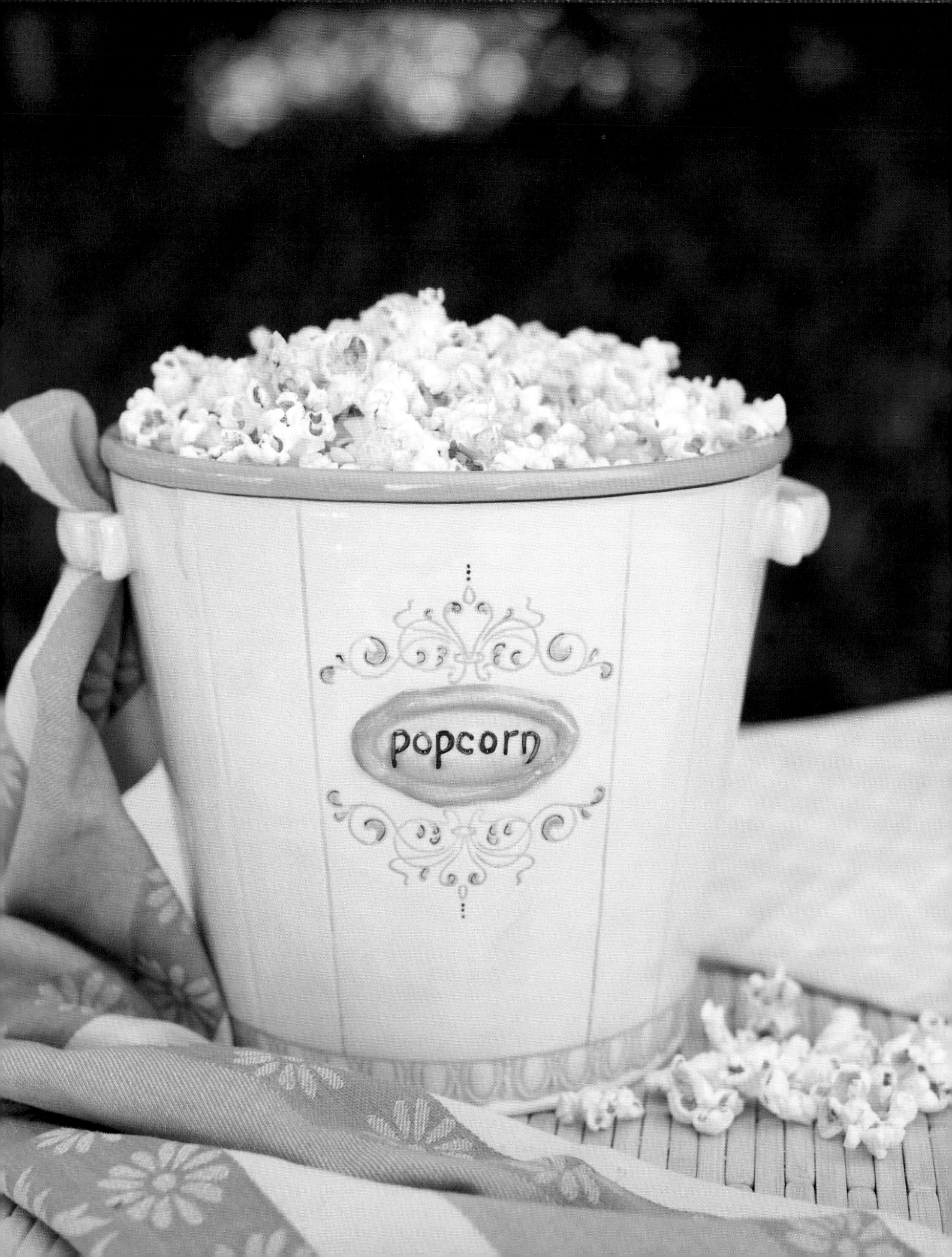
popcorn

Popcorn

10 C of popped corn (air popped)

3 Tbs or more of extra light olive oil

2 - 3 Tbs of nutritional yeast flakes or to taste

Make popcorn sufficient to make about 10 C of popped corn in an air popper.
Drizzle extra light olive oil over the popped corn, salt to taste, and sprinkle nutritional yeast flakes over all. Very tasty.

Nutrition Facts (1 serving = 1/3 recipe)

Calories 204, Fat 13 g, Saturated 2 g, Polyunsaturated 2 g, Monounsaturated 9 g, Trans fat 0 g, Cholesterol 0 mg, Sodium 3 g, Carbohydrate 19 g, Dietary fiber 5 g, Protein 6 g, Vitamin A 1 %, Vitamin C 0%, Calcium 1%, Iron 6 %

Pesto Pizza

Pesto Sauce for One Pizza

½ C toasted pine nuts or walnuts

1 - 2 cloves of garlic, crushed

2 C fresh basil

1/3 C extra virgin olive oil

½ tsp salt

Blend all ingredients in the blender. You can use this on pizza, with pasta, or on a sandwich. Serves 4 - 6. Nutrition Facts for sauce: Serving size = 1 serving, servings per recipe 5, calories 240, calories from fat 219, fat 24 g, saturated 3 g, cholesterol 0 mg, sodium 221 mg, carbohydrate 3 g, dietary fiber 1 g, protein 5 g, Vitamin A 4%, Vitamin C 4%, Calcium 2%, Iron 11%.

Pizza Crust Made in Bread Machine—Makes 2 Crusts

1 1/3 C whole wheat flour

1 1/3 C unbleached flour

2 Tbs vital wheat gluten

1 tsp salt

1 ½ tsp Italian seasoning

2 Tbs honey

2 Tbs olive oil

1 C warm water

1 ½ tsp yeast

Mix dry ingredients. In bread machine put the honey, olive oil, warm water and then add the flour mixture. Even the flour out and make a well in the center and add the yeast. Close the lid and set machine on the dough cycle. This makes 2 crusts. When the cycle is finished take enough dough to make one crust and you can freeze the rest of it. Spread the dough on the pizza pan, poke the center of the crust with a fork in several places so it won't puff up and then bake just the crust for 10–15 minutes at 375 degrees until the crust starts to brown. Then take it out of the oven, spread the pesto sauce on the crust. Top with sliced tomatoes, sliced green olives, sliced black olives, sliced artichoke hearts, chopped onions and then you can sprinkle Parmazaan (optional) on top. Return the pizza to the oven for 10–15 minutes or until done.

Nutrition Facts (1 slice = 1/16 recipe)
Calories 98, Fat 2 g, Saturated 0 g, Trans fat 0 g, Cholesterol 0 mg, Sodium 147 mg, Carbohydrate 18 g, Dietary fiber 2 g, Protein 3 g, Vitamin A 1%, Vitamin C 1%, Calcium 1%, Iron 6%

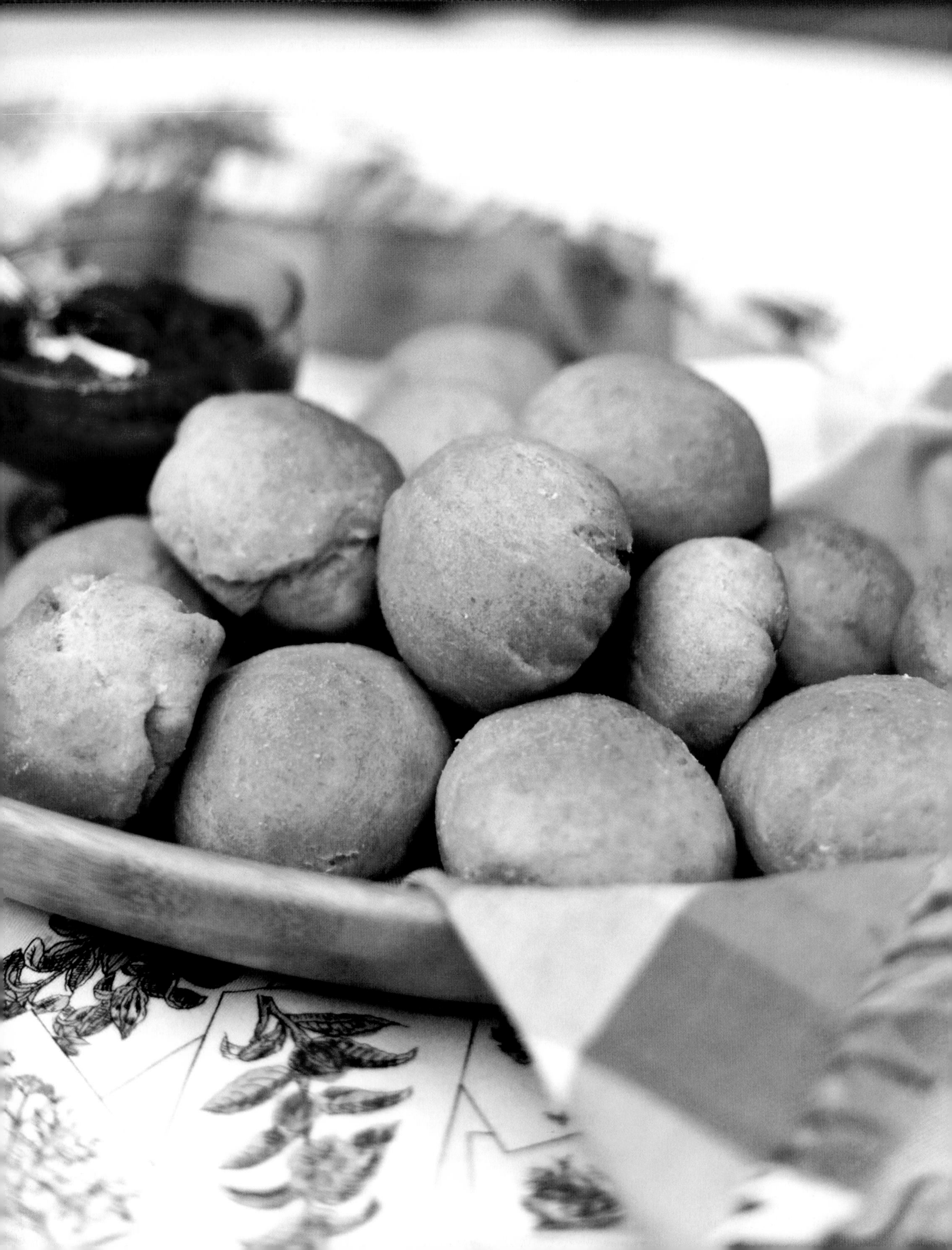

Dinner Rolls

(Using a Bread Machine)

2 C white wheat flour

1 C unbleached flour or bread flour

1 C white rye flour

3 Tbs vital wheat gluten

2 ¼ tsp salt

2 ¼ tsp yeast

1 ½ C warm water

3 Tbs honey

3 Tbs olive oil

Mix flours, vital wheat gluten, and salt in bowl. Put the water, honey, and oil into the bread pan. Then add the flour mixture, making a little well in the center, and put the yeast in the well. Close lid and put machine on the dough cycle. When cycle is finished, divide the dough into 12 evenly sized pieces and shape into rolls and place on a cookie sheet sprayed with Pam. Bake at 350° for about 20 minutes or until golden brown.

Yields: one dozen dinner rolls.

Nutrition Facts (1 roll)

Calories 191, Calories from fat 38, Fat 4 g, Saturated 1 g, Cholesterol 0 mg, Sodium 415 mg, Carbohydrate 34 g, Dietary fiber 4 g, Sugars 0 g, Protein 6 g, Vitamin A 0%, Vitamin C 0%, Calcium 1%, Iron 9%

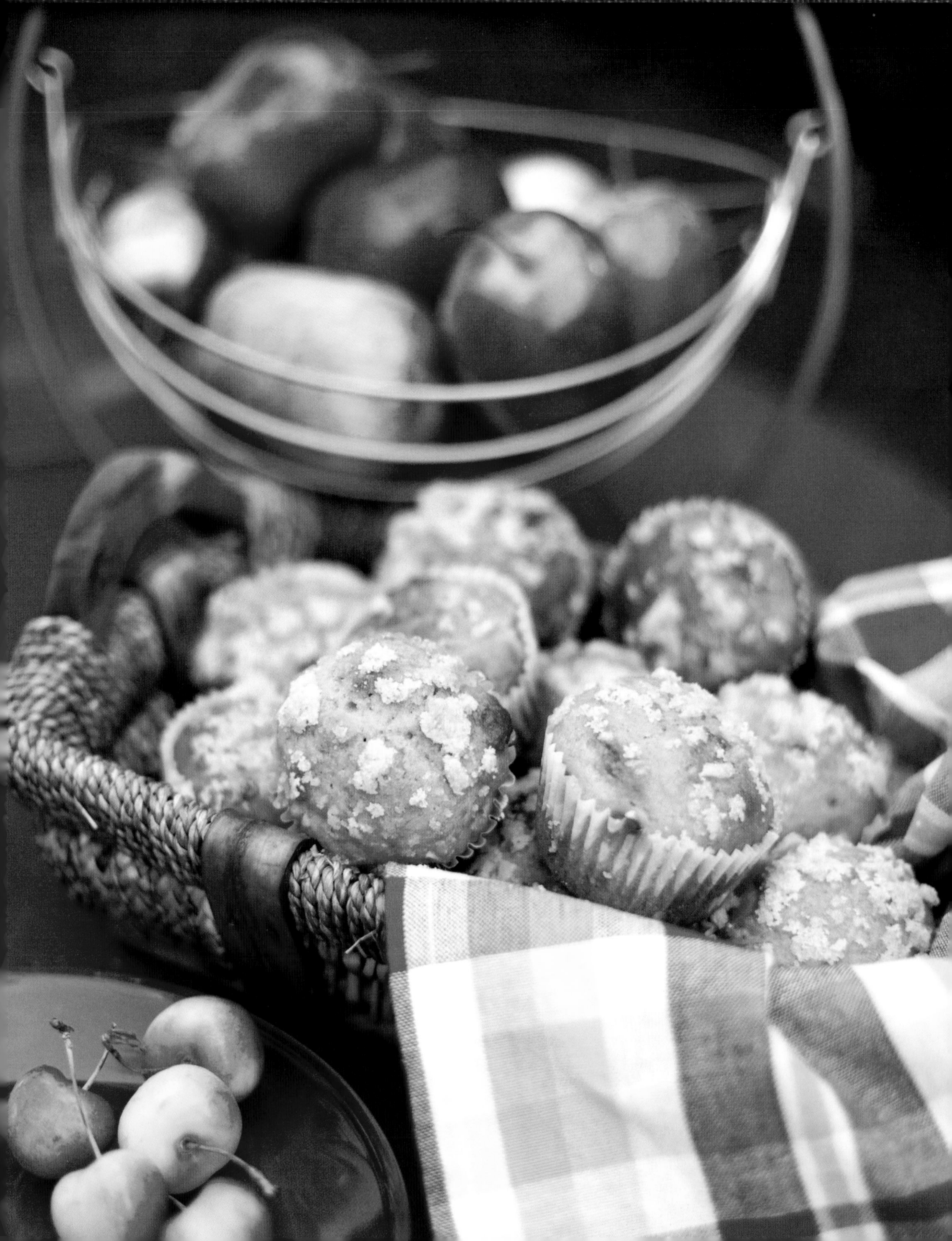

Apple-Walnut Muffins

1 ½ C unbleached flour

½ C whole wheat pastry flour

1 ½ tsp Rumford baking powder

¼ tsp salt

½ tsp cinnamon

¼ tsp nutmeg

1 C soymilk

½ tsp vanilla

1 C maple syrup

¼ C extra light olive oil

1 small unpeeled apple

½ C walnuts, chopped

Preheat oven to 375°. Mix the dry ingredients well. Then mix the soymilk, maple syrup, olive oil, and vanilla. Add the liquid ingredients to the flour mixture and stir well. Fold in the chopped apples and chopped walnuts. Fill the cups of a 12 C muffin tin about 2/3 full. Bake for 20 - 25 minutes. Leave in the muffin tin for 5 minutes and then remove the muffins and put them on a cooling rack. (Optional topping for the muffins: 2 - 3 Tbs unbleached flour, 2 Tbs sucanat, ½ tsp cinnamon, 1 Tbs extra light olive oil. Mix with a fork until crumbly and put on top the muffins before baking them.

Nutrition Facts (1 serving = 1 muffin)

Calories 233, Fat 8 g, Saturated 1 g, Polyunsaturated 3 g, Monounsaturated 4 g, Trans fat 0 g, Cholesterol 0 mg, Sodium 173 mg, Carbohydrate 37 g, Dietary fiber 2 g, Protein 4 g, Vitamin A 2%, Vitamin C 2%, Calcium 12%, Iron 10%

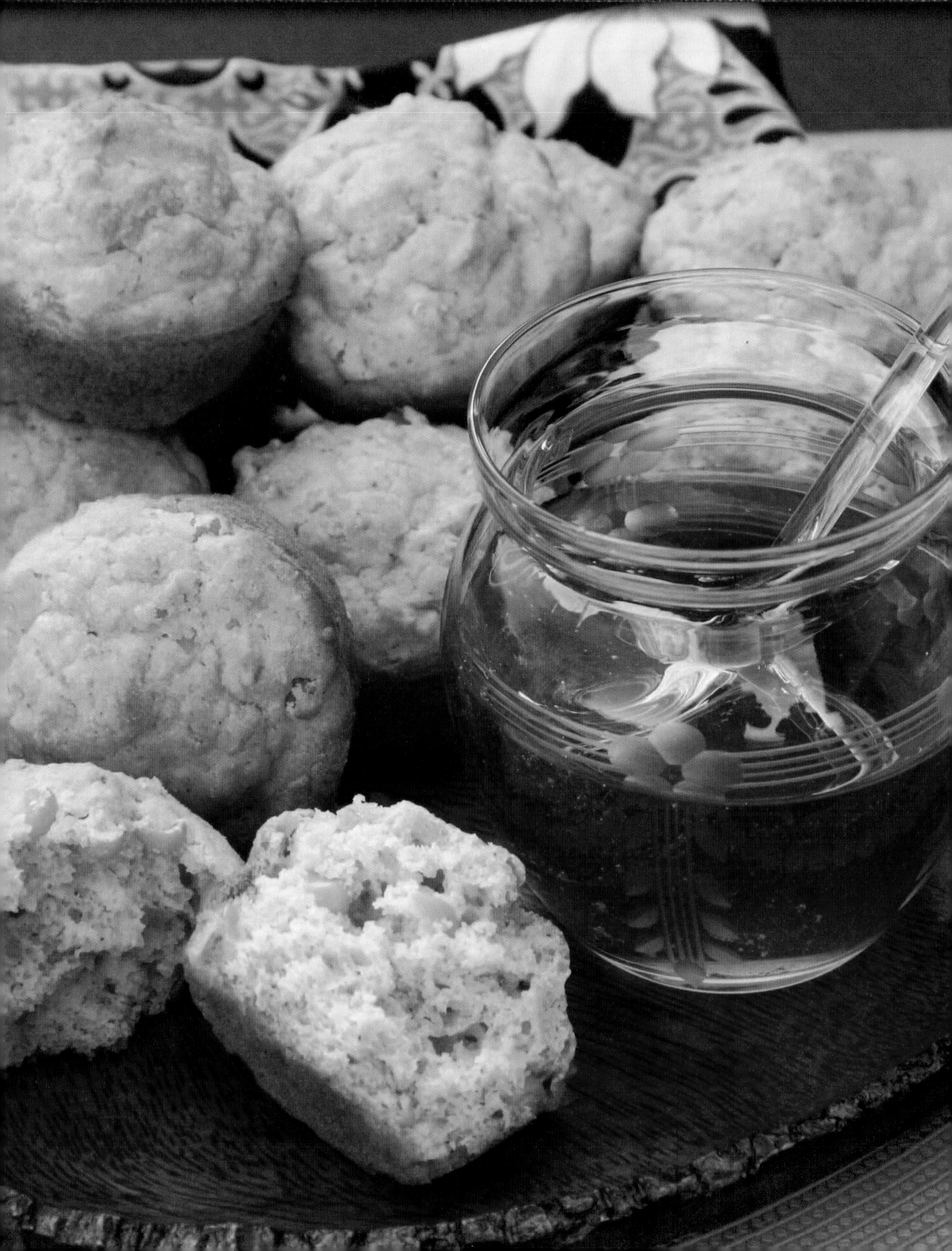

Cornbread Muffins

1 C unbleached flour

1 C cornmeal

2 Tbs Rumford baking powder

2 Tbs sucanat

½ tsp salt

Ener-G egg replacer for 1 egg

1 can creamed corn

2 Tbs melted Earth Balance margarine

½ C soymilk with ½ Tbs lemon juice added to make buttermilk

Mix the flour, cornmeal, baking powder, sucanat, and salt. Follow the directions to make the equivalent of one egg with the egg replacer. Take the ½ C soymilk and add the lemon juice and let it sit for about 5 minutes, then stir. This will make buttermilk.

In another bowl put the creamed corn, egg replacer, soymilk, and melted margarine and mix well. Now add the liquid ingredients to the flour mixture and stir well. Oil a muffin pan and fill with the batter. Bake for 25 minutes at 375° or until lightly browned. Serve with Earth Balance margarine and honey. Very yummy!

Makes 12 muffins.

Nutrition Facts (1 muffin)

Calories 130, Fat 3 g, Saturated 1 g, Polyunsaturated 1 g, Monounsaturated 1 g, Trans fat 0 g, Cholesterol 0 mg, Sodium 668 mg, Carbohydrate 25 g, Dietary fiber 2 g, Protein 3 g, Vitamin A 1%, Vitamin C 3%, Calcium 34%, Iron 7%

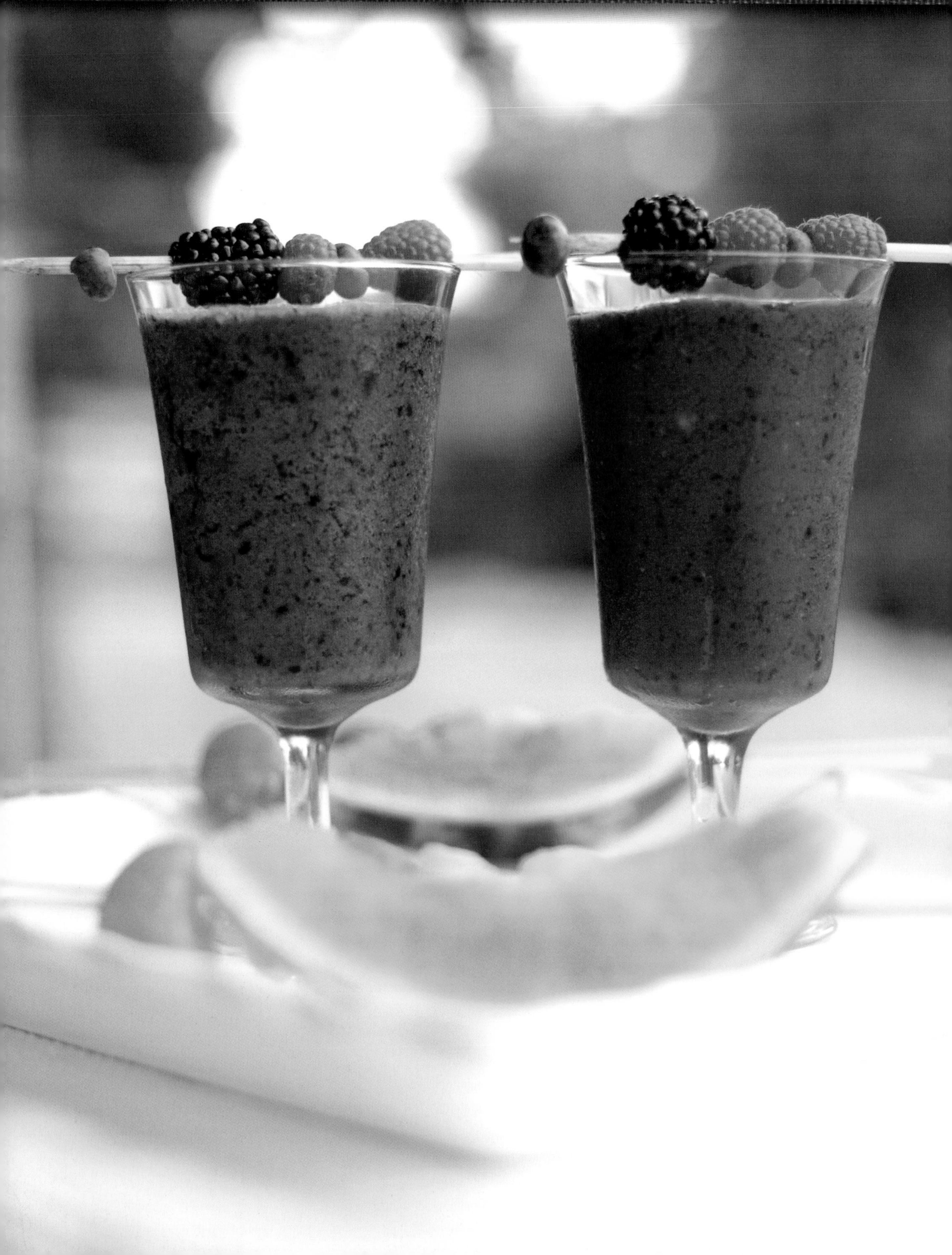

Fruit Smoothies

1 banana, frozen in chunks

½ C frozen strawberries

½ C frozen blueberries

½ C frozen raspberries

1 - 1 ½ C soymilk

1 Tbs pure maple syrup (optional)

Blend all ingredients in blender. Serves 3.

Nutrition Facts (1 serving = 1/3 recipe)
Calories 120, Fat 2 g, Saturated 0 g,
Trans fat 0 g, Cholesterol 0 mg,
Sodium 57 mg, Carbohydrate 22 g,
Dietary fiber 5 g, Protein 6 g, Vitamin A 5%,
Vitamin C 29%, Calcium 6%, Iron 10%

Cappuccino

2 cups Silk vanilla soymilk

2 tablespoons maple syrup

2 teaspoons powdered coffee substitute (Roma or Pero)

½ teaspoon vanilla extract

Briefly blend all ingredients in the blender. Serve hot or chilled.
Makes 2 servings.

Hint: You can top with whipped topping and a sprinkle of cinnamon.
This recipe is from the cookbook *The Total Vegetarian,* by Barbara Watson.

Nutrition Facts (per 8-oz serving)

Calories 179 , Protein 9.2 g,

Carbohydrates 25.7 g, Dietary fiber 3.2 g,

Fat 5.1 g, Sodium 32 mg

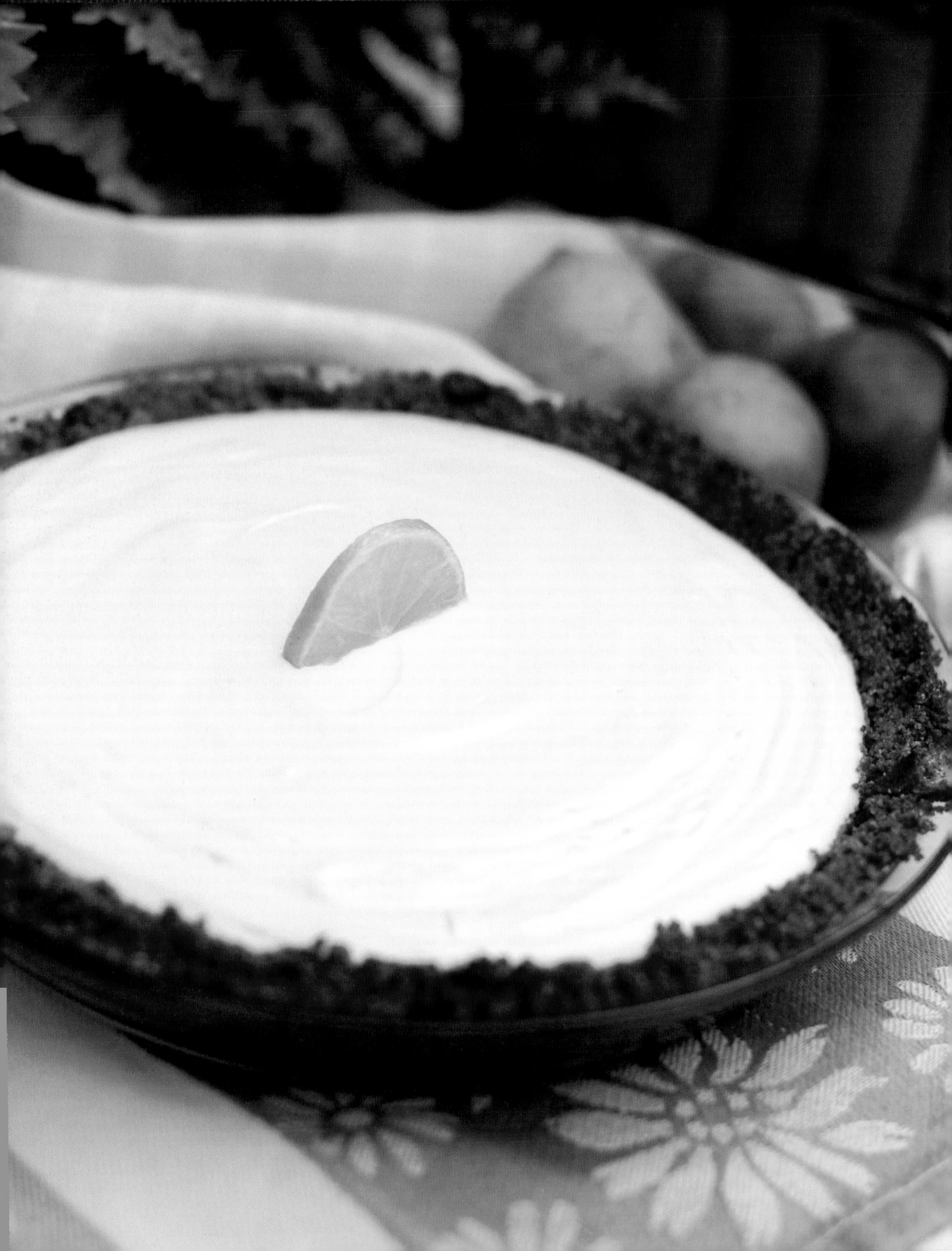

Key Lime Pie

Pie Filling

1 8-oz Better Than Cream Cheese

½ C lime juice (can use lemon if you don't have limes)

2 pkg Mori-nu mates lemon crème pudding mix

1 Tbs honey

1 pkg Mori-nu light extra-firm tofu

2 Tbs sucanat

Blend in blender and pour into graham cracker crust.

Graham Cracker Crust

1 ½ C graham crackers, crushed

2 Tbs extra light olive oil

4 Tbs pure maple syrup

Mix ingredients together until well combined. Then press mixture into the bottom and up the sides of a 9-in pie plate or tin.

Hint: Arrowhead Mills makes a graham cracker crust that's free of trans fats.

Nutrition Facts (1 slice = 1/8 pie)
Calories 351, Fat 18 g, Saturated 5 g,
Trans fat 0 g, Cholesterol 0 mg,
Sodium 280 mg, Carbohydrate 42 g,
Dietary fiber 1 g, Protein 5 g, Vitamin A 1%,
Vitamin C 2%, Calcium 3%, Iron 6%

Date Bars

Outer Layers

1 ½ C whole wheat pastry flour

1 ½ C quick oats

½ tsp salt

½ C chopped walnuts

1 - 2 Tbs water

½ C extra light olive oil

½ C sucanat

Date Filling

2 ½ C pitted dates

2 ½ C water

Combine flour, oats, salt, water, and walnuts. In a separate bowl mix the olive oil and sucanat. Add the olive oil mixture to the flour. Press half of the mixture into the baking dish. Cook the dates in the water until they can be mashed into a paste. Let the dates cool. Spread the date paste over the crumb mixture. Then spread the rest of the crumb mixture over the dates and press it gently. Bake at 350° for 25 minutes. Makes about 25 bars.

Nutrition Facts (1 serving = 1 bar)

Calories 159, Fat 6 g, Saturated 1 g, Polyunsaturated 1 g Monounsaturated 4 g Trans fat 0 g, Cholesterol 0 mg, Sodium 48 mg, Carbohydrate 26 g, Dietary fiber 3 g, Sugars 15 g, Protein 3 g, Vitamin A 1%, Vitamin C 1%, Calcium 2%, Iron 5%

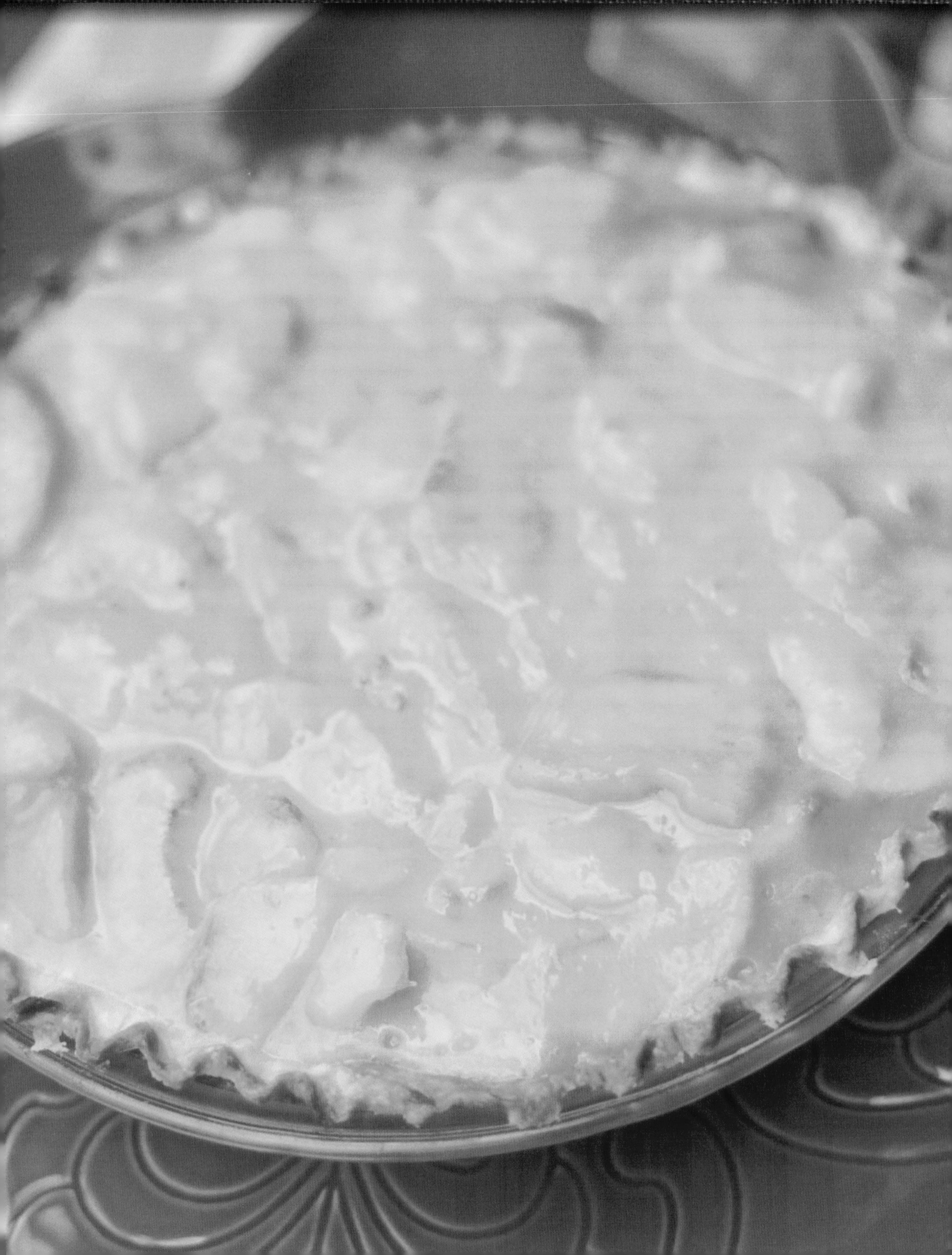

Fresh Peach Pie

1 9-in single pie crust, baked

4 oz Better Than Cream Cheese, softened

¾ C sucanat

6 ½ C firm-ripe peaches, sliced, peeled

¾ C orange juice

1/3 C cornstarch

1 Tbs lemon juice

Mix Better Than Cream Cheese with ¼ C sucanat until smooth. Spread evenly over cooled, baked pie crust. In blender whirl 1 C sliced peaches, remaining ½ C fructose, orange juice, and cornstarch until smooth. Pour into kettle and cook over medium-high heat until it boils and thickens. Remove from heat and stir in lemon juice.

Add remaining peaches to hot peach glaze and gently mix to coat slices. Let cool. Pour peach mixture onto cream cheese in pie crust. Refrigerate.

Serving Tip: Chill uncovered until firm enough to cut—at least 3 hours. Serve with whipped topping flavored with orange zest.

Nutrition Facts (1 slice = 1/8 pie)

Calories 300, Fat 11 g, Saturated Fat 2 g, Polyunsaturated 4 g, Monounsaturated 5 g, Trans fat 0 g, Cholesterol 0 mg, Sodium 214 mg, Carbohydrate 49 g, Dietary fiber 3 g, Protein 4 g, Vitamin A 4%, Vitamin C 25%, Calcium 2%, Iron 6%

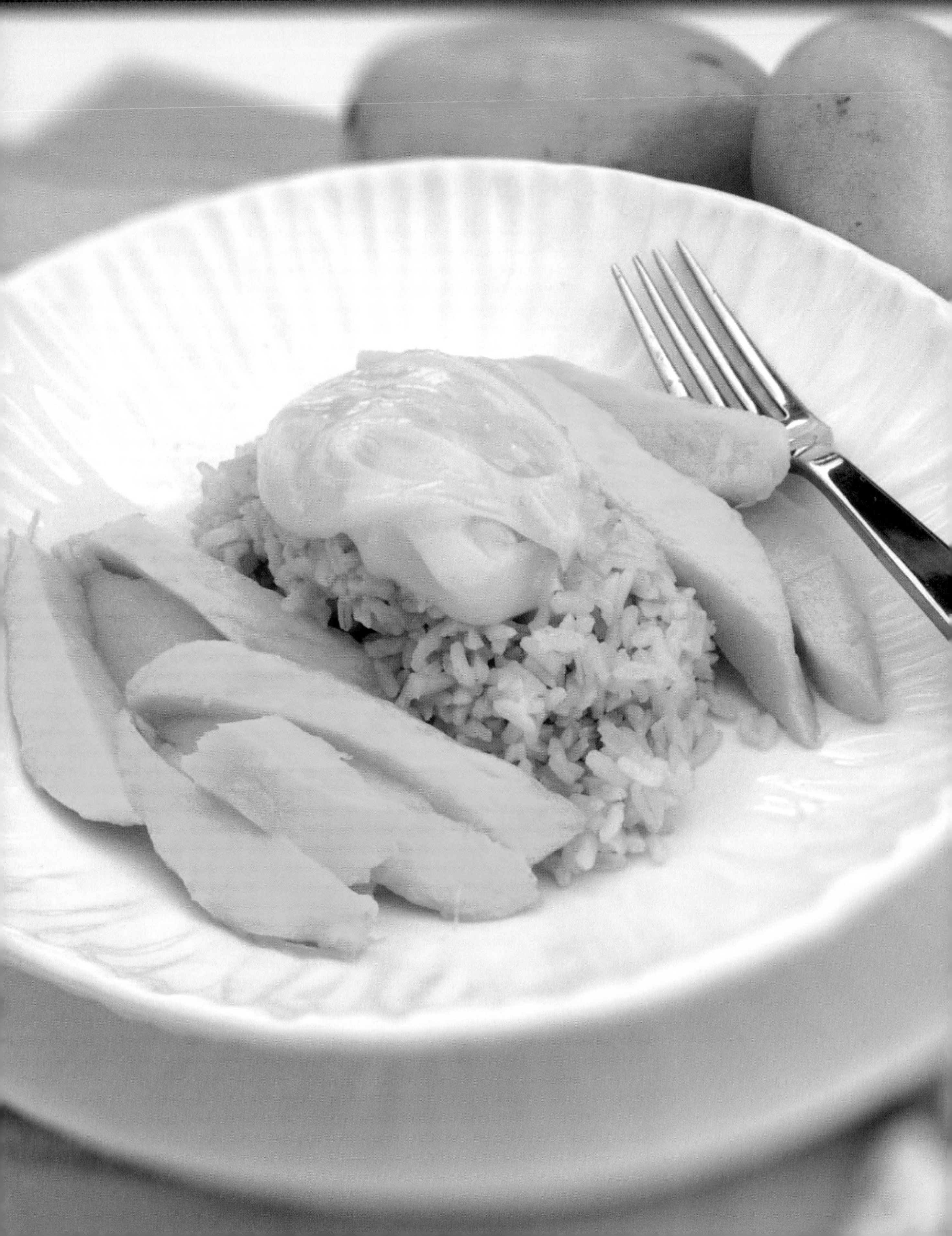

Mangos & Sticky Rice

2 C jasmine brown rice

½ C sucanat

1 can coconut milk

2 mangos, peeled, pitted

Put rice in a strainer and wash until the water is clear. Then put the rice in a bowl and cover with cold water and let it soak overnight or 8 hours or more. Then cook the rice until tender.

Heat the coconut milk in a kettle and add the sucanat. Bring to a boil and stir. Reduce heat, cover, and simmer for about 5 minutes until slightly thickened.

Pour coconut milk over the rice and fluff with a fork. Cover and let it sit for 15 minutes. Scoop a mound of rice onto each plate and serve with fresh sliced mangos. Serves 4.

Hint: Before serving, you can add some cream of coconut—about 1/3 C—to the rice. It makes it more sticky and sweet. Very yummy! Cream of coconut can be found in Asian markets.

Nutrition Facts (1 serving = ¼ recipe)
Calories 583, Fat 12 g, Saturated 7 g,
Trans fat 0 g, Cholesterol 0 mg,
Sodium 17 mg, Carbohydrate 113 g,
Dietary fiber 5 g, Protein 8 g, Vitamin A 23%,
Vitamin C 38%

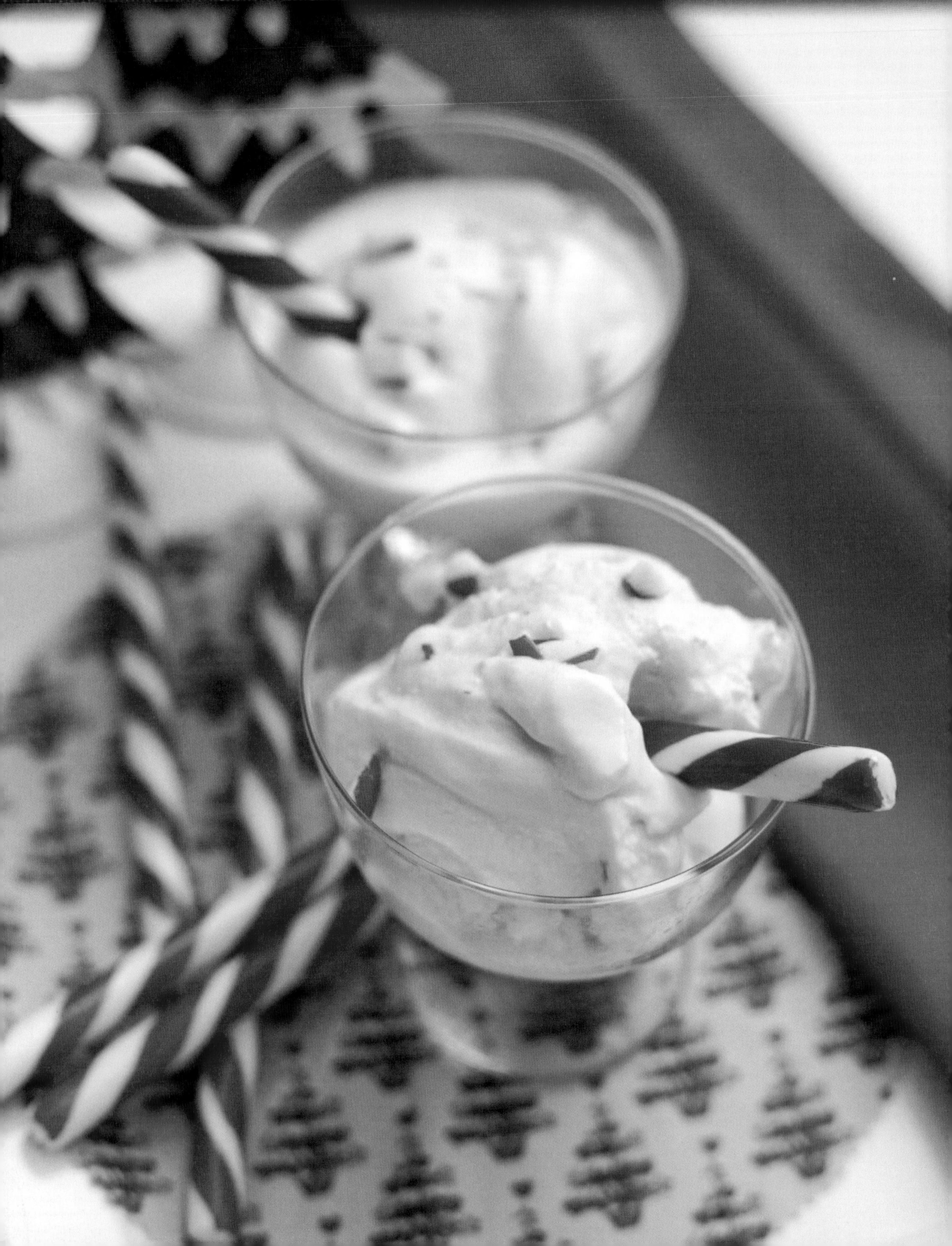

Peppermint Ice Cream

2 pts soy creamer or Mimic Cream

½ - 1 tsp peppermint extract

½ C sucanat

Pinch of salt

½ peppermint stick, crushed

Mix the soy creamer, extract, sucanat, and salt in a pitcher and refrigerate. When you're ready to make the ice cream, pour it into the frozen tub and turn the machine on. After the ice cream is beginning to thicken, add the crushed peppermint candy (you will only need ½ - 1 whole peppermint stick for one batch of ice cream).

This is a fun ice cream to make for the holidays.

Nutrition Facts (1 serving = 1/9 recipe)

Calories 111, Fat 7, Saturated 0 g,
Trans fat 0 g, Cholesterol 0 mg,
Sodium 87 mg, Carbohydrate 18 g,
Dietary fiber 0 g, Protein 0 g, Vitamin A 0%,
Vitamin C 0%, Calcium 1%, Iron 1%

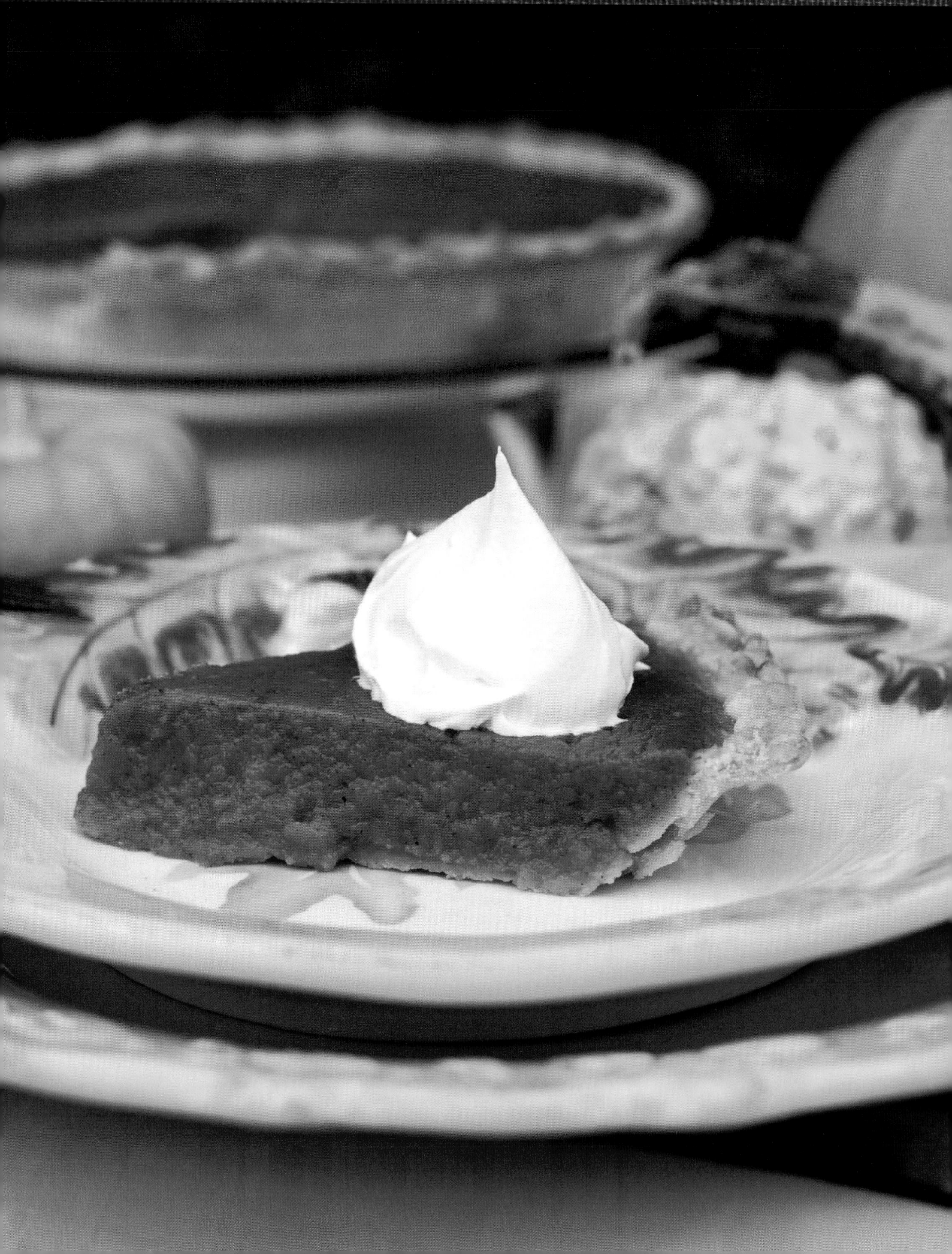

Pumpkin Pie

1 14-oz can pureed pumpkin

1 C vanilla soymilk

½ C pure maple syrup

½ C sucanat

3 Tbs cornstarch

½ tsp salt

½ tsp cinnamon

1 tsp pumpkin pie spice

1 unbaked pie crust

Mix canned pumpkin, soymilk, maple syrup, sucanat, cornstarch, salt, and spices. You can blend in blender or mix with an electric mixer. Pour into an unbaked pie shell and bake for 1 hour in a preheated oven of 350°. Let the pie cool on a cooling rack before refrigerating. The pie will get more firm as it cools. Top with non-dairy whipped topping. Serves 8.

Nutrition Facts (1 serving = 1/8 pie)
Calories 254, Fat 8g, Trans fat 0 g,
Cholesterol 0 mg, Sodium 431 mg,
Carbohydrate 46 g, Dietary fiber 3 g,
Protein 3 g, Vitamin A 57%, Vitamin C 3%,
Calcium 9%, Iron 15%

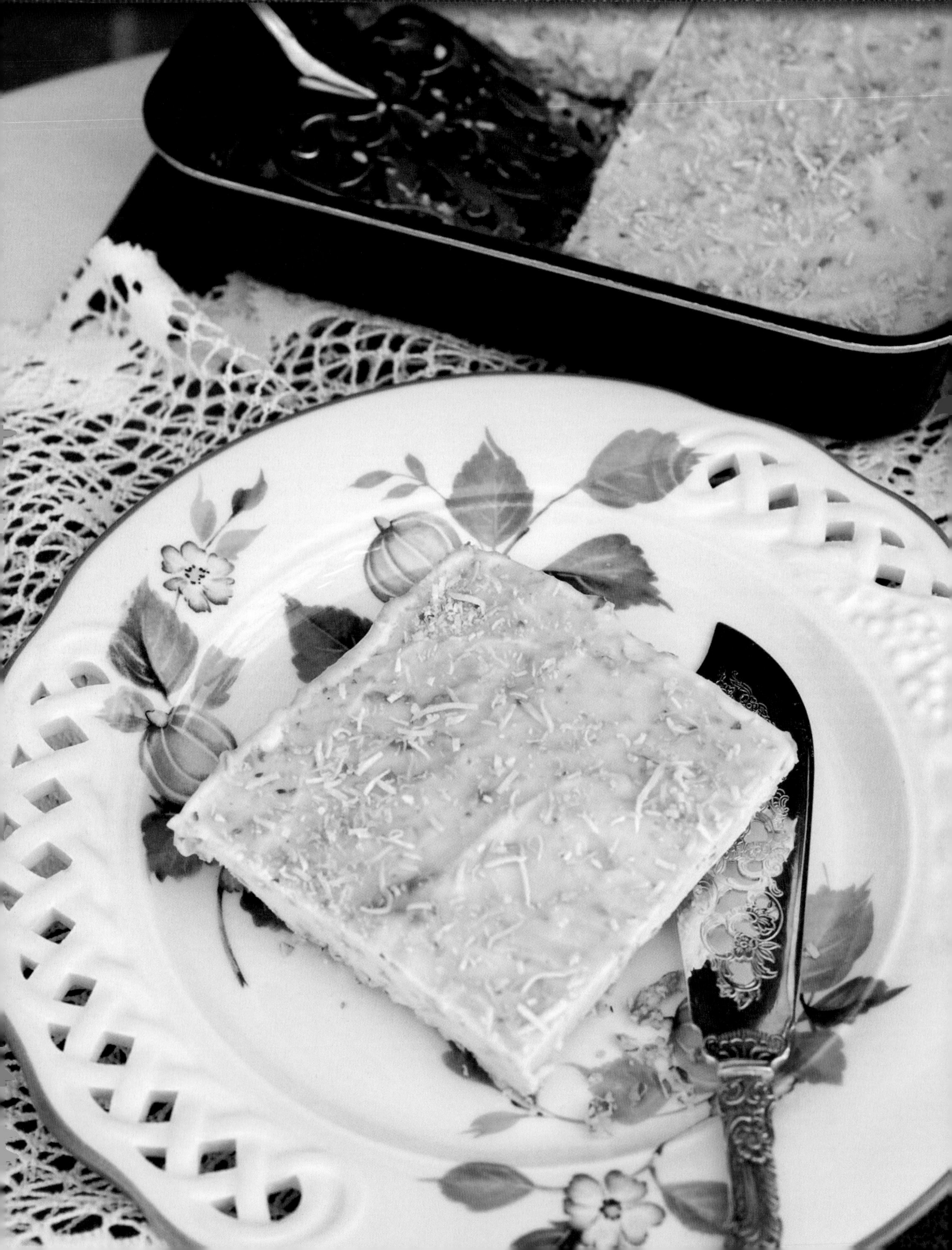

Almond Delight Ice Cream Pie

Almond Crust

1 ½ C toasted almonds, chopped

1 Tbs extra light olive oil

1 ½ Tbs honey

Coat an 8 x 8-in pan with non-stick spray. Mix the crust ingredients and press the mixture firmly onto the bottom and sides of the pan. Then put the pan in the freezer and freeze while preparing the filling.

Filling

¼ C unsweetened, finely shredded coconut, lightly toasted

1 Tbs honey

½ C almond or peanut butter

3 Tbs toasted almonds, chopped

2 pints vanilla soy ice cream

In a small bowl mix the coconut, honey, almond butter, and almonds. Place the ice cream in a large bowl and stir to soften. Stir in the almond mixture. Spoon into the chilled crust. Sprinkle additional toasted coconut over pie. Freeze for at least 2 hours or until firm. You can cut the pieces to whatever size you wish, so you can serve anywhere from 8 - 12. This recipe is from *Depression, the Way Out*.

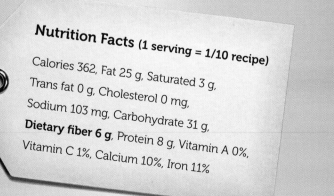

Nutrition Facts (1 serving = 1/10 recipe)

Calories 362, Fat 25 g, Saturated 3 g, Trans fat 0 g, Cholesterol 0 mg, Sodium 103 mg, Carbohydrate 31 g, **Dietary fiber 6 g**, Protein 8 g, Vitamin A 0%, Vitamin C 1%, Calcium 10%, Iron 11%

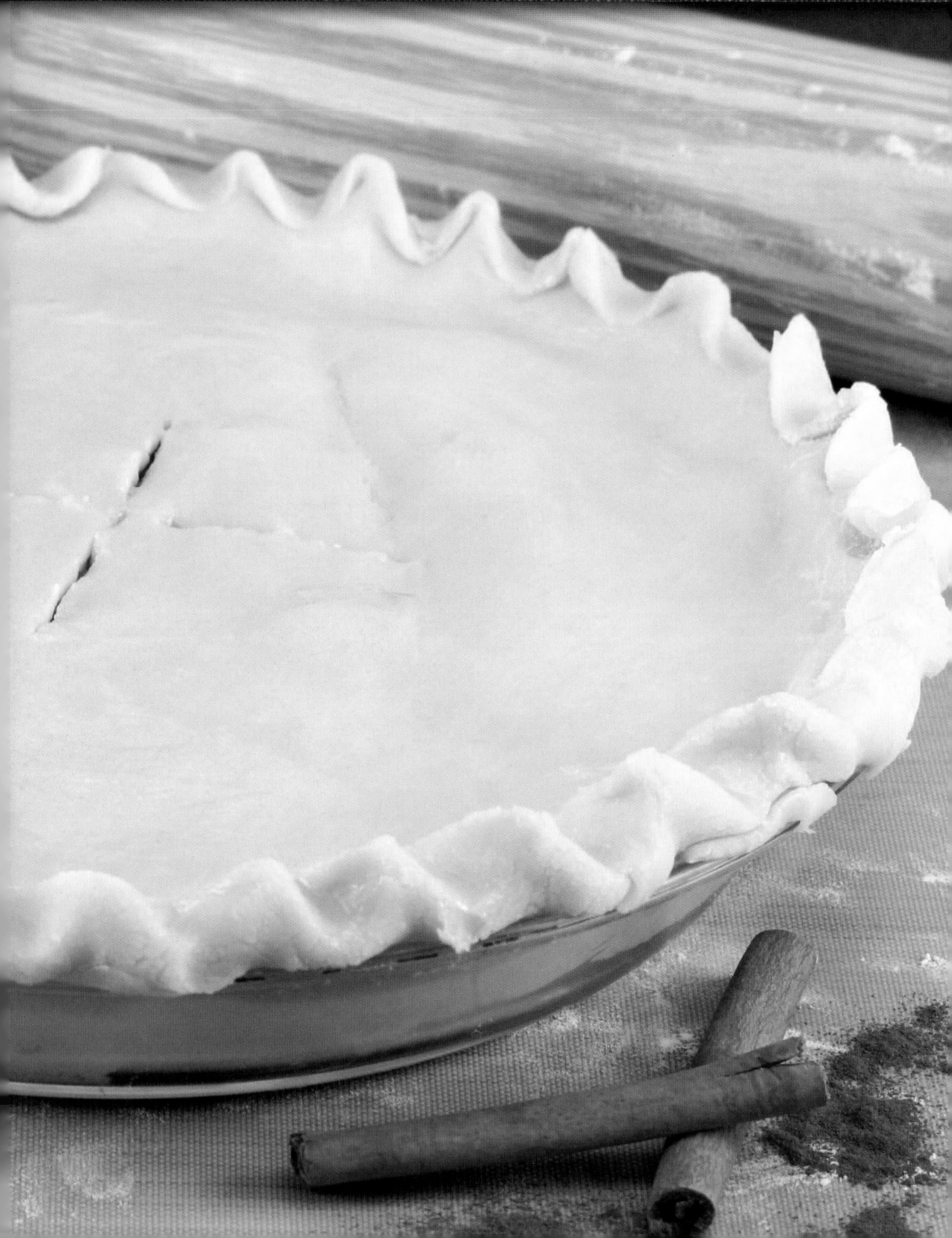

Pie Crust

1 C unbleached flour

1 C whole wheat pastry flour

1/2 C extra light olive oil

1 tsp salt

½ C boiling water

Mix salt and flour. Pour water and oil in, all at once. Stir with a fork. Roll between 2 sheets of waxed paper. Remove top paper. Lay crust side down. After putting the top crust on the pie, flute the edges. This is a double pie crust. Bake as pie recipe indicates.

Hint: You can vary the whole wheat pastry flour to use more or less, as long as the total flour measurement comes to 2 cups.

Nutrition Facts (1 serving = 1/8 recipe)

Calories 225, Fat 14 g, Saturated 2 g, Polyunsaturated 2 g, Monounsaturated 10 g, Trans fat 0 g, Cholesterol 0 mg, Sodium 292 mg, Carbohydrate 23 g, Dietary fiber 2 g, Protein 4 g, Vitamin A 0%, Vitamin C 0%, Calcium 2%, Iron 8%

Product Info

Better Than Cream Cheese Made by Tofutti, this is a soy-based cream cheese substitute that works well in any recipe calling for cream cheese. Be sure you get the non-hydrogenated kind.

Better Than Sour Cream This is also made by Tofutti and is a soy-based sour cream with no cholesterol. Look for the non-hydrogenated kind.

Bragg's Liquid Aminos This is a liquid soy protein that seasons food. It's lower in sodium than soy sauce. Found in a health food store. Can be used in place of soy sauce.

Desserts You will notice I have a section for desserts in this book. We try to limit our desserts to once a week. I usually make a fruit pie of some type. Most of the desserts have about 3 gm of fiber per serving, so at least you are getting some fiber in it. Try to keep your desserts to a minimum, and when you do make them, enjoy to the max!

Double Fiber Bread Oroweat makes a bread called "Double Fiber" that has 6 gms of fiber per slice. When making sandwiches or fruit on toast, this is a great way to boost your fiber intake. One sandwich with this bread gives you 12 gms of fiber, as opposed to 4 gms with regular whole grain bread.

Egg Replacer, Ener-G Used in baking to replace eggs. It's made from starch. You can find it at a health food store.

Honey You will notice that I have used honey in some of my recipes. If you prefer not to use honey, substitute with pure maple syrup.

Instant Food Thickener A corn starch thickener that can be added to foods without cooking the food. Made by Diamond Crystal. Phone number 800-227-4455.

Margarine If you use margarine, Earth Balance is a brand that is non-hydrogenated and has good flavor. Read the label on Smart Balance, some of their varieties have whey in them, which is a milk product.

Mimic Cream This is a creamer made from nuts and can be used when making home-made ice cream. It is found in the refrigerator section of your health food store or can be ordered on the Internet at www.mimiccream.org.

Misto Sprayer An air pump olive oil sprayer that can be ordered on the Internet.

Non-Dairy Whipped Topping One brand, Soyatoo, makes Soy Whip, found in the freezer section of the health food store. This whipped topping is vegan. Truwhip is another brand available at health food stores that is 70% organic and has no hydrogenated oils—it has less than 2% of a milk product in it. Truwhip is a better choice over other mainstream brands.

Olive Oil Extra virgin olive oil is the oil of choice. It's loaded with antioxidants and is the only oil I use. I use the extra virgin oil for salad dressings and to sauté foods. I use the extra light olive oil for baking, because I don't want the olive taste in some foods. Studies have shown that olive oil actually helps with memory by binding with toxins that promote Alzheimer's disease.[1]

1. *Toxicology and Applied Pharmacology*, volume 240, Issue 2, Oct. 2009.

Dairy Free Cheese There are several brands to choose from. Tofutti brand makes a casein free cheese in slices and there's also a new brand our called "Daiya", it is made from tapioca and is gluten free. "Daiya" brand comes shredded.

Parma Zaan Sprinkles This is a replacement for parmesan cheese. It has no oxidized cholesterol. Produced by The Vegetarian Express—phone number 734-355-3593. They also have a ranch seasoning you can use to add to Vegenaise if you choose not to make your own ranch salad dressing.

Rumford Baking Powder This baking powder doesn't have any aluminum in it. You want to avoid aluminum, as it contributes to Alzheimer's disease.

Soymilk I prefer to use the unsweetened soymilk. It has very few ingredients in it and cuts down on calories, as well.

Sucanat Sugar **ca**ne **nat**ural (dehydrated cane juice). This is a natural sweetener. It is not as refined as white sugar and not bleached. Also comes in the grocery store under the brand "Florida Crystals." Be sure to get the white variety, not the brown, especially when making the soy ice cream.

Stevia This is an herb often called "sweet leaf." It usually comes in powder form, and only a small amount is needed to sweeten your food. Stevia is essentially calorie free, and the body processes it slowly, so it doesn't cause a spike in blood sugar. It doesn't work for every recipe, but when it can be used, it's a great natural sweetener.

Tortilla Wraps La Tortilla brand wraps are wonderful. They are loaded with fiber—12 - 13 gms in each wrap. When making your veggie wraps, look for this brand. Most health food stores carry them, and even some grocery stores have them.

Vegenaise A tasty, non-dairy mayonaise that's found in the refrigerator section of a health food store. It has no cholesterol.

Vegetarian Chicken or Beef Seasoning There are three brands to choose from— McKay's, Bill's Best, or Vegetarian Express. Most health food stores have McKay's seasonings, although some of their seasonings have milk or whey in them. You would have to ask to order the vegan variety.

Vital Wheat Gluten Also known as Do-Pep, this is a high-gluten flour used to make gluten steaks or added to bread to give it a nice consistency.

Vegex or Savorex Yeast extract used as a flavor enhancer. It can be found in health food stores.

Yeast The best yeast I've found for bread making is Saf-Instant. It comes in a 16-oz size and lasts a long time. Once I open it, I freeze it and just use it as needed. You can usually find this in a health food store.

THE FOLLOWING TRADEMARKED™ AND / OR REGISTERED® PRODUCT BRAND NAMES ARE USED IN THIS BOOK: Pam cooking spray, McKay's chicken style seasoning, Bill's Best, Rumford baking powder, Vitamix, Blendtec, Morningstar Farms products, Lawry's, Mrs. Dash, Vegenaise, Better Than Sour Cream, Better Than Cream Cheese, Bubbie's pickles, Frontier Mexican seasoning, Tony's seasoning, Campbell's Healthy Request soups, Spike seasoning, Pepperidge Farm, Worthington FriChik, La Tortilla, Do-Pep, Vegex, Savorex, Cedar Lake, Ener-G Foods, Tofutti, Barilla, Bragg's Liquid Aminos, Earth Balance margarine, Silk soymilk, Roma, Pero, Mori-nu Mates pudding mixes, Soyatoo, Diamond Crystal, Mimic Cream, Oroweat Double Fiber, Truwhip, Parma Zaan Sprinkles, Saf-Instant, and Misto

Gift Baskets

Extending yourself to someone by taking them a home-made gift can strengthen friendships, or even make new friends. Through the years, I have taken a loaf of home-made bread to new neighbors who have moved into the area. The response has always been very positive. On one occasion, the neighbors had just moved here and didn't know anyone. Dan and I walked over and knocked on their door. The lady opened the door and saw me standing there with the loaf of bread in my hands, and she threw her arms open and welcomed me with a hug! We became fast friends and now are even best of friends.

Get Well Basket

When you know of someone who has become ill—particularly someone who lives alone and has no one to look after them—a basket filled with health-promoting foods is a welcome sight. You can fill the basket with fresh fruit, home-made bread, nuts, fruit juice, etc.

Banana Bread

If you want to take a loaf of banana bread to your neighbor, you can make it look really special in the way you present it. At various craft stores you can find boxes and fancy lace paper or tissue paper—and then adding a fresh flower or two makes it even more appealing.

Simple Gifts

Sometimes you just want to let someone know you are thinking of them. A simple home-made gift of granola, date bars, fresh nuts, a little pie, or whatever it is you make that day can brighten up someone else's life. I always keep some small pie plates on hand, so that when I'm making a pie for our family I can make a little extra for someone else.

Christmas Basket

A Christmas basket is fun to do. When making a basket for a family, I usually like to make a large pot of soup. I try to label the items in the basket so people can know what they're getting. Of course, with the soup goes a loaf of home-made bread. I put the bread in a plastic bag and then tie raffia around it and put in some sprigs of wheat on the top. Sometimes I will put a label or a gift tag on the bread.

A small box of crackers goes well with soup. Then add a bottle of sparkling juice. And hanging a Christmas tree ornament over it makes it more festive. I load the basket with fresh fruit and slip a kitchen towel through the handle of the basket. A small green plant adds color—or a little flowering plant. I usually include a dessert, and you can even put a serving plate to go with it. This basket is filled with a meal they can enjoy and is packed with love from you.

Food is something everyone can enjoy, and home-made food is even better. God bless you as you share with others and are a blessing to them.

Gardening

Growing a garden and having fruit trees is a major blessing. It doesn't matter if you have a small yard or not, you can still plant a tree somewhere. My husband thinks that my goal is to cover every inch of our property with fruit trees! Well, he's close to right! There's nothing like growing your own fruits and vegetables. You know what you're getting. You don't have to deal with pesticides or chemicals.

If you live in a city or apartment and don't have the ability to grow trees or plant a garden, you can have an herb garden in your house or sprout some seeds to add to your salads and sandwiches. You can grow something, wherever you live.

Not only do you benefit from your fruit being free of chemicals, you are outdoors in the sunlight, breathing fresh air and soaking up some Vitamin D from the sun. If you worry that bending down will cause those aches and pains, make a box garden, or you can buy them ready made. You will enjoy watching the plants grow or the seeds sprout, and seeing the fruit grow on the trees reminds you of our Creator and how He has bountifully blessed us.

Your children and grandchildren will love the garden and trees. That's the first place our grand-babies, Callie and Joshua, want to go—down in the grove to pick some peaches, plums, citrus, or whatever happens to be ready at the time. This last year, Dan and I picked 500 pounds of avocados—our first real crop. We enjoyed picking them ourselves.

You can take some of your fruit, if you have an abundance, and dehydrate it, or we freeze the peaches and apples. I freeze my apples in 6 C measurements so that if I want to make a pie, they are all sliced and ready to go. Sharing with friends is fun too.

Whatever you do, if you plant something, enjoy it to the max. God has promised to bless "the fruit of your land"—Deuteronomy 7:13.

Recommended Resources

Twenty Four Realistic Ways to Improve Your Health by Dr. Tim Arnott. This is an awesome little book that's packed with valuable information on simple ways you can stay healthy. I can't recommend this book enough to you.

Depression, the Way Out by Dr. Neil Nedley. If you or someone you know suffers from depression, this book is an excellent resource. It shows how you can overcome depression the natural way.

The Best of Silver Hills Cookbook by Eileen Brewer. I've used recipes from this cookbook in my cooking classes. They are great recipes and good for you too. Eileen has a new cookbook out called *Silver Hills Spa Cuisine*.

The Total Vegetarian by Barbara Watson. Another cookbook I've used in my classes that has tasty, health-promoting recipes.

The Vegetarian Express This company provides seasonings such as the Parma Zaan cheese—a substitute for parmesan cheese. They carry a ranch seasoning that you just add to Vegenaise for a salad dressing. You can order by phone and have it shipped to you, or some health food stores carry their products. Phone number: 734-355-3593.

Health Power by Dr. Aileen Ludington & Dr. Hans Diehl. This book shares simple lifestyle changes that can be made to improve your health. They show step by step how many lifestyle diseases can be prevented, reversed, and even cured by changes nearly everyone can make at home.

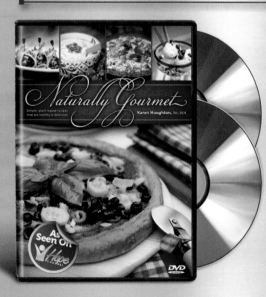

Naturally Gourmet™
Cooking Series on DVD

If you like this cookbook, you'll love cooking along with host, **Karen Houghton** on the popular series featured on the **Hope Channel**. This DVD set contains 14 shows with 7 hours of heart-healthy programming!

Dr. Wes Youngberg co-hosts each episode. He brings a wealth of information with healthy facts from the latest medical studies.

To order your copy, visit www.NaturallyGourmet.com!